STRENGTH FOR TODAY

FOR TEEN GUYS

365
DEVOTIONS

BroadStreet
PUBLISHING

BroadStreet Publishing
Savage, Minnesota, USA

STRENGTH FOR TODAY FOR TEEN GUYS

© 2022 by BroadStreet Publishing®

9781424565092
9781424565108 (e-book)

Devotional entries composed by Jared Winger.

Design by Garborg Design Works | garborgdesign.com
Editorial services by Michelle Winger and Carole Holdahl.

Printed in China.

22 23 24 25 26 27 28 7 6 5 4 3 2 1

INTRODUCTION

You can walk in confidence when you rely on God to be your strength. Be encouraged with truth as you spend time with God, reflecting on these devotions, Scriptures, and prayers. As you spend time with him, he will fill you with courage and hope for each day.

Let your heavenly Father show you that, through him, even in your weakest moments, you are significant, and you are strong. Find your purpose in God and be ready to conquer each day!

ESTABLISHED

In their hearts humans plan their course,
But the LORD establishes their steps.
PROVERBS 16:9 NIV

We all dream about taking our abilities to the next level. There is nothing wrong with a desire to become great. In fact, God would encourage strong desires that lead to positive pursuits. However, we want to be aligning ourselves with his plans as our first priority. He made us and knows what we are best equipped for. When we make and follow our own plans without involving God, pride or shame trip us up. But when we confidently follow God's plans, we can know that he is guiding us. When execution goes well or it falls apart, we are not prideful or ashamed because we have followed God, and he is leading us.

Know that God wants you to be next level. He will give you all you need to walk according to the plans he has for you.

Father, help me to plan according to your will and in all things please you. Guide my steps this year as I walk with you.

CAPABLE AND CARING

When you ask, you must believe and not doubt,
because the one who doubts is like a wave of the sea,
blown and tossed by the wind.

JAMES 1:6 NIV

One of the hardest things we face is peer pressure. Try as we might, it is really difficult to stand up against a crowd and speak for what we believe in. We can be influenced to say and act in manners that we never intended because we want to be part of a group. Ultimately, we just want to belong.

The same things happens when we question whether or not we are God's children. Does he hear us and does he even care? Jesus encourages us that he certainly does care, and he does hear. He wants us to ask the Father with assurance that we will be answered, and that our tiny faith will be rewarded. We belong to him, and as a part of his tribe we are taken care of by the biggest, most powerful, capable, and caring Being in the universe.

Jesus, I am encouraged to ask you for all that I need today because you care for me. I am part of your family.

OVERCOME WITH GRATITUDE

His bow remained steady,
his strong arms stayed limber,
because of the hand of the Mighty One of Jacob,
because of the Shepherd, the Rock of Israel.

GENESIS 49:24 NIV

This verse is about Joseph, an Old Testament example of the nature of Christ. In his youth, Joseph was boastful and overly confident in himself. But as he aged, he demonstrated the steadfastness of God. He faced brothers who wanted him dead and sold him as a slave. He was confronted with incredible temptation and was unjustly imprisoned. Yet, in all these things he trusted God and was faithful to him.

Why, when he went through so much, was Joseph able to be godly? Well, that was entirely because he kept God at the center of his life. Joseph's focus was on God and not on his circumstances. He prayed, he praised, he was thankful, and he believed. Ultimately, his trust in God led him to become a prince of Egypt. God is mighty and strong to uphold us in all seasons of life.

God, help me to look to you and not be overwhelmed by what I feel. Fill me with gratitude and praise.

HONESTY WITH FEELINGS

"Don't be afraid, for I am with you.
Don't be discouraged, for I am your God.
I will strengthen you and help you.
I will hold you up with my victorious right hand."
ISAIAH 41:10 NLT

Have you thought about what makes you afraid? Is it external like physical pain, the behavior of certain people, or just you and your friends doing crazy things? Maybe it is mostly internal like thoughts and feelings. Perhaps you are afraid of what others think of you. Shame drives the feeling that others may not like us or that we are somehow not worth knowing. Shame comes from Satan. God dislikes shame. He wants us to be fearless around him and know that we are loved and accepted.

God is faithful to keep you close to him and he will always love you no matter what you are going through. What he wants from you is honesty and openness with him. Keep yourself open to God and allow him to see all the things you want to hide. Ask for forgiveness when you need it, and trust that he loves you. Fear not!

Father, help me to be open and honest with you. Thank you for your forgiveness. I ask that you would encourage me to follow you and walk with you without fear.

CHILL OUT

"Abide in Me, and I in you. As the branch cannot bear fruit itself,
unless it abides in the vine, neither can you, unless you abide in Me."
JOHN 15:4 NKJV

When do you find yourself talking differently or acting in ways that
you may not have before? Usually it is when you hang out with certain
groups of people. If you think about how you acted a few years ago, what
has changed? What do you do more or less of now? Likely you changed
the way you were because you were hanging out with a particular group
of people, and you started acting like they act. This is normal human
behavior.

Jesus knew people imitated those they hung out with. This was why
he was calling his disciples to dwell with him. He knew the more they
gathered together, the more like him they would be. He wasn't asking
them to learn the Bible and then take a test. He wasn't asking them to
memorize facts about him. He was telling them to chill, rest, be, and
dwell with him.

*Jesus, help me learn to be with you, and not just to learn about you. I want
my life to be like yours. I want to hang out together and hear from you.*

LEADERSHIP

In those days Israel had no king;
everyone did as they saw fit.
JUDGES 21:25 NIV

Not long ago, there was trouble afoot in Africa when young elephant bulls were rampaging, destroying nature, and killing other animals including fellow elephants. Poachers had killed the older male elephants, so there was no one to keep the young males in check. Once the rangers recognized this, they introduced some mature bull elephants and peace was restored.

When leadership is lacking, people will do what they want, casting aside consideration of others and only caring about themselves. They will steal, loot, destroy, and even kill without remorse. As Christians, we always have a King. He never leaves us, nor does he forsake us, and we do not want to rebel against him because he is good, righteous, just, and true.

Lord, I commit my heart to be led by you, and I ask that you would show me where my life is not submitted to you. Help me to be your servant in a wicked and self-serving world. I want to love others and show them how good you are.

IN THE FACE OF FAILURE

Being fully assured that what God had promised,
He was able also to perform.
ROMANS 4:21 NASB

It is easy to be confident when we come up against competition that we think we can beat. When we do, we are usually confident because of our practice record, skill level, natural talent, and so forth. But what do we do when we recognize our weaknesses? How can we be confident then? Confidence in the face of failure and inability can only happen because of some outside force. Perhaps we are on a team of good players? That was what Abraham felt like when he was told to do things that he knew he could not do. He trusted his team, which was God alone. His faith was what enabled him to do things that only could be done through the power of God.

You are no different, and God says that even when you are weak, he will be your strength. Trust in him to help you do things you are both skilled at and things that you feel overwhelmed by. Be full of faith, knowing that God is with you.

Father, help me to believe in you. Give me the faith that Abraham had to do the impossible. I want to live my life in obedience to all that you ask me to do.

HOPEFUL

We rejoice in our sufferings, knowing that suffering produces endurance,
and endurance produces character, and character produces hope.
ROMANS 5:3-4 ESV

It is good to look at the words of this verse and understand the way we
can be moved forward from suffering to hope. We all suffer, some of us
more than others. And when we do, we can become overwhelmed by our
situation. But this verse encourages us all to not be overwhelmed; we can
have hope. If this is true— that our suffering produces hope— then we
can rejoice in it. All of this can happen when we place God at our center,
draw close to him, and dwell upon his Word.

You are not alone in what you suffer, and through Christ you can actually
find a new hope. But also notice that this verse is plural; it is that *we*
rejoice in *our* sufferings. Together with other people who believe, you can
overcome and have hope.

*God, help me to be with other Christians who encourage me to be thankful,
to push through difficulty, and to be strengthened in you. I want to learn
how to overcome and to be filled with hope.*

ALIVE

"Whoever drinks of the water that I shall give him will never thirst.
But the water that I shall give him will become in him a fountain of water
springing up into everlasting life."

JOHN 4:14 NKJV

Have you ever been so thirsty that when you finally drank water, it was like the best thing you ever tasted? Your body needs water. Dehydration causes your body to conserve water. Kidneys send less water to your bladder and that makes darker urine. Your blood thickens, making your heart work harder to keep up the oxygen levels. All of this happens for the lack of a few drops of water.

Jesus knew what he was talking about when he equated a connection from himself to everlasting water. Just like water is critical to life, if we don't remain connected to him, our spirits weaken and die. He is our sole provider, and he sustains our life.

Jesus, help me to drink from your everlasting water. I want to remain connected to you so that I am alive and in full strength for the great things that you have for me to do.

MY DEFENDER

All Scripture is inspired by God and is useful for teaching,
for showing people what is wrong in their lives, for correcting faults,
and for teaching how to live right.

2 TIMOTHY 3:16 NCV

It is not fun to be corrected. It is even harder when someone corrects you and you already know you did something wrong, like when you are feeling convicted by God's Word and then someone also points out your wrongdoing. The reality is, that this conviction and the resulting repentance, is good for us. God says that he lifts up the humble, and that the repentant heart produces good fruit.

Ultimately, if you are reading this, you are a person who wants to follow Jesus, so you are willing to receive his Word and be corrected by it. Let this encourage you today, and when you are shown your fault in some matter, admit it and humble yourself as Christ would.

Jesus, like you, I want to be humble. Help me to receive correction from others and not allow my pride and self-defense to get in the way. You are my defender and I trust in you.

UNDERSTOOD

We do not have a high priest who is unable to sympathize with our weaknesses,
but one who in every respect has been tempted as we are, yet without sin.
HEBREWS 4:15 ESV

Think about God and his power. With his word he created the earth and all its inhabitants. Think about all he can see and understand. So many things are beyond our comprehension. He is a marvel, unparalleled to men. Yet he agreed to leave his place of power and authority and become what he created! Wow. He humbled himself so much that he became as weak as men. He didn't need to do this to understand us because he made us. He did it to show us his power over sin and death; he did it to free us from Satan. Now as God-man, seated in heaven, he fully understands our plight; he sees our weaknesses and our temptations. He prays for us.

You can be full of confidence because Jesus knows all you are experiencing. He has lived it. He also has the power to change you and your circumstances! You need not fear anything with him on your side!

Jesus, thank you for knowing me and my experiences. I ask for your help with confidence that you will faithfully and powerfully meet me where I am.

THE VOICE OF THE SPIRIT

"You will receive power
when the Holy Spirit comes on you."
ACTS 1:8 NIV

Have you ever been shocked by electricity? It is not a fun experience when that kind of power is conducted through you. It is why they call it shocking! The disciples were not expecting electricity, fire, or wind when they sat in prayer awaiting the Holy Spirit after Jesus died and was resurrected. But when he came it was a powerful experience. They even expressed the experience in ways that make us think their senses were being overwhelmed; buzzing, on-fire, pulsing, ecstatic, and awakened!

They were fully alive and engaged with God when the Holy Spirit came, and their lives were forever changed. He wasn't a shock that came and left. He stays with us and connects us directly to God the Father. The Holy Spirit wants to be an integral part of your daily life: guiding, leading, comforting, and teaching you all things.

Holy Spirit, thank you for being here with me. I ask today that you fill me with your presence and lead me so that I may draw closer to the Father. Help me to hear your voice.

BOLD

"Why are you frightened?" he asked. "Why are your hearts filled with doubt?
Look at my hands. Look at my feet. You can see that it's really me. Touch me and
make sure that I am not a ghost, because ghosts don't have bodies, as you see
that I do." As he spoke, he showed them his hands and his feet.

LUKE 24:38-40 NLT

Fear drives us to do things we normally would not do. If a lion appeared behind you as you read this, what would you do to get away? Everything and anything! When Jesus appeared, the disciples shrank back in fear. That is why he invited them to come to him, touch him, and affirm that he was real. He told them he would be resurrected, and he was.

After overcoming their anxieties, they were elated to realize it was really him. It affirmed their faith, and they were emboldened to share with others. Beating fear will give you bravery.

Jesus, help me to see you and to be in touch with you so that I can be brave. Give me your words to share and help me to encourage others to love you.

SPEAKING WITHOUT GOSSIP

You can't trust a gossiper with a secret;
they'll just go blab it all.
Put your confidence instead in a trusted friend,
for he will be faithful to keep it in confidence.
PROVERBS 11:13 TPT

How easy it is to listen to someone's story about another person. It's juicy information that makes us want to know more. We are all storytellers, and some of the best tales come through gossip. We watch social media and share stories without thinking about what harm they may do. How can we be people of honor when we relish the rubbish of society? How can we give value to the stories that mean nothing and have no basis in truth?

Your best way to grow in honesty, righteousness, faithfulness, and truth is to set aside tales about others. Focus instead on speaking truth. Only repeat what you know. The gospel is truth, and the Bible is full of stories that you can confidently share.

Father, help me to be a man of truth, to share what I know, and to only repeat what I know is founded in compassion. I want to honor you and others with the way I speak.

POVERTY AND PLENTY

*I know what it is to be in need, and I know what it is to have plenty.
I have learned the secret of being content in any and every situation,
whether well fed or hungry, whether living in plenty or in want.*
PHILIPPIANS 4:12 NIV

If you listed all the painful and difficult things Paul went through, you would find out that he was a man who was full of endurance. He knew what it was like to go through something hard and to continue on regardless. Because of this, he also understood what it meant to have little or lots. Imagine driving the greatest car and having a huge house and lots of money, then losing it all and having nothing but the clothes on your back. Paul knew this but was always thankful. Why? Because it wasn't about this life right now. He understood that God had so much more for him.

You too, have much more in Christ. It is about what Jesus has given you now through salvation, and what he has in store for you later in eternity.

*Jesus, help me to set my heart on your kingdom and not on this world.
Fill me with desire for the things that you care about.*

LIKENESS

Give freely and become more wealthy;
be stingy and lose everything.
The generous will prosper;
those who refresh others will themselves be refreshed.

PROVERBS 11:24-25 NLT

God's kingdom is upside down compared to this world. He wants us to serve, but this world promotes the idea that each of us is the boss. He wants us to give generously and to care for others, but this world teaches us to put ourselves first and to make ourselves happy. To be first in this life is good, but to be last in God's kingdom is better. This world tells us to do something because it feels good. But God asks us to do the hard things and be patient for the sake of his kingdom. He desires that men be strong, controlled, and not led by their immediate desires. What a crazy kingdom compared to this world!

In this faith, you learn to constantly challenge the message of the world and to renew your mind in Christ. As you read his Word you will understand his heart and be more like him. You are no longer shaped by this world, but by his Sprit in you!

Holy Spirit, teach me the ways of God and help me to be conformed to the likeness of Jesus Christ.

DO IT

By grace you have been saved through faith.
And this is not your own doing; it is the gift of God.
EPHESIANS 2:8 ESV

Sometimes we don't like being told what to do. We like to do things ourselves. The worst is when you go to do something good for your parents, say, clean up the dishes or take out the trash, and they tell you to do it before you get the chance to take the initiative. *Grr.* That is so annoying. I t is not unusual for us to want to do something good and make it on our own. We want to be independent.

God says that you must depend upon him. He says that it is good for you to believe him and not try to do anything more to be saved. He has saved you, and because of your faith in him you are made right with God. Keep that faith strong and believe that it is a gift to you.

God, thank you so much for saving me and giving me the faith to believe in you. Help me in my unbelief and fill me with joy and thankfulness for what you have done.

GUARDIAN

"Well did Isaiah prophesy of you hypocrites, as it is written, 'This people honors me with their lips, but their heart is far from me; in vain do they worship me, teaching as doctrines the commandments of men.' You leave the commandment of God and hold to the tradition of men."

MARK 7:6-8 ESV

As we develop, our brains form greater connections, and we understand things on a deeper level. We are able to think abstractly and take up oppositional arguments to our own thinking. But this doesn't take place immediately in our adolescent years. During our teens, our brains are starker. We think more in black and white, and we take up causes that we don't fully understand. We don't see or comprehend the gray. As we grow, we have to be wary about taking up causes that don't please God.

As a young person, guard your heart and mind so that you will be able to determine the will of God, and do not be persuaded by the opinions of men. God will watch over you in this formative time as you submit your life to him. Allow his Word to guide your mindset.

Father, I don't want to become religious and unyielding. Guard my heart and the issues I allow it to be concerned with. I want to demonstrate your character not the rules and declarations of men.

STORYTIME

We will not hide these truths from our children;
we will tell the next generation
about the glorious deeds of the LORD,
about his power and his mighty wonders.

PSALM 78:4 NLT

The Bible is made up of many stories that were eventually recorded in written form. These stories were handed down to each generation through storytelling and song. We still do this today in various forms of media. Movies, especially, give us a visual, emotional, and auditory connection to a story that allows us to obtain a deeper sense of a message or tale. God has given us incredible minds to hear, store, and recall wonderful stories, pictures, and dreams. He intends for those to entice us toward knowing him more. His tales are honest, real, connecting, and inviting.

You are a part of his story, and he wants to share more with you. He wants you to remember his goodness and power so that in whatever circumstances you face, you will have faith in him.

God, help me to recall your wonderful deeds and to be reminded of your character and goodness in all that you do. I want to know you more and to tell those around me about you.

DIFFICULT THINGS

He shepherded them according to the integrity of his heart,
And guided them with his skillful hands.
PSALM 78:72 NASB

A shepherd can do things that could cause loss or harm to the sheep or their owner. He can be negligent by taking naps, allowing the sheep to wander into danger; or he could decide to not fight for them when they face trouble. We also have situations in our workplaces that could do harm. We could hurt others or ourselves if we steal, cause damage, or are careless. But Jesus is not this way. He has integrity of heart and is focused and diligent in what he does. He calls us to be the same, whether we are working for a person, a company, a church, or doing things for him.

In all things he asks you to be honest, hard-working, attentive, and disciplined. It is a challenging call. Most likely you will stand out as different but be encouraged that when you walk this way and work this way there are rewards both on earth and in heaven. Employers will want you to work for them. Jesus will increase your abilities and reward you.

Jesus, thank you for being a good shepherd. Please lead me to walk in your ways and to do the hard things regardless of how others are acting.

FOLLOWER

Your obedience is known to all, so that I rejoice over you,
but I want you to be wise as to what is good and innocent as to what is evil.
ROMANS 16:19 ESV

What a great thing to be known for— obedience to God. A person who strives for this and achieves it regularly is a disciplined person who has no other idols in their life. Often our idols are subtle; we can seek first for gratification through media, sports, hobbies, etc. All of them can take the place of God in our lives and lessen our desire to remain disciplined and obedient. This is why he follows up his sentence with the statement that we should know what is good and not dwell on what is evil. This is similar to saying that we should keep our eyes on the things above and not on the world below.

You are made to pursue God passionately and fully. You can fix your eyes on him, and he will guide you into truth and a deeper knowledge of him.

Thank you, God, for keeping me on your path. Help me to obey you and follow after your commands with all of my heart.

JANUARY 22

HEALING

"I will restore you to health and heal your wounds," declares the LORD.
JEREMIAH 30:17 NIV

God is our healer. The Hebrew name given to him in this definition is *Jehovah- Rapha*, meaning "the Lord who heals." But sometimes we see those around us get sick and even die. You may ask yourself, "Why if you are the healer, God, do you allow people to die? Why do so many stay sick?"

This is not God's desire or design. Sin is why we face sickness and death. Yet at times God chooses, by his mercy, to interrupt normal life and bring healing. Jesus came into our world to break these curses. He made a way for us to live forever and to be healed. Ultimately, those of us who choose him will be healed of all sickness and disease, and we will dwell forever with him on a newly made planet without sickness or other curses! By faith, you can confidently ask for him to heal you and others, which he will do in his timing.

Father, please heal me of my sicknesses, and prepare me for resurrection when you return. Fill me with faith to see healing take place in this life, though I know ultimately all will be healed in the next life.

GOD SIGHTING

The LORD is all I need, he takes care of me.
My share in life has been pleasant;
my part has been beautiful.
PSALM 16:5-6 NCV

How often do you see God taking care of you? When we were children in Sunday school, teachers would ask us to look for God moments in our lives, where God was present and seen in day-to-day activities. We would come back reporting many. Sometimes as we get older, we forget to marvel at how much God is interacting with us.

He may speak through his Word, a friend, a stranger, an answer to prayer, or a sense of his presence. He is very personal and wants us to know his constant closeness through the person of the Holy Spirit. Today, be encouraged that he is with you, and that as you take time to look for him, he will be found. God promises to meet with you when you seek him out.

God, I want to see you today in whatever activity I am doing. Open my eyes to you.

LOVING AS JESUS DOES

God demonstrates his own love for us in this:
While we were still sinners, Christ died for us.
ROMANS 5:8 NIV

Can you imagine a bully or someone who hates you asking for you to do something to help them? The obvious answer is, "No, I will not help you." An even more difficult scenario to imagine would be them asking you to die in order to save them. That would be illogical and ridiculous. Who would do such a thing?

Jesus would! All of humanity was an enemy of God. Our sins and our practices were despised by him. Yet God sent Jesus to become a man, to suffer, and then to die at the hands of men in order to save humanity. What an incredible demonstration of love. It is why Jesus said that we must even love our enemies and those who hate us. This kind of love is beyond feelings. It is found only in Christ, and it is through Jesus that we can love this way. You have Christ in you, and he can teach you to love this way. Ask him, and he will be faithful to answer you.

Jesus, help me to love others like you do. Help me to look beyond myself and my needs to show your character to others.

GREAT THINGS

I will remember the deeds of the LORD;
yes, I will remember your miracles of long ago.
I will consider all your works and meditate on all your mighty deeds.
PSALM 77:11-12 NIV

Have you ever been excited about Christmas? Of course you have! What gets us excited about Christmas is the emotions and the memories of the years before. We have learned to be excited from what we have remembered. In this Psalm, the writer is encouraging the same recall of great things because he was discouraged. He was considering the awesomeness of God so that he would be full of faith to overcome the problems he was facing at that time.

God is faithful and powerful enough to help us through any difficulty. Remembering what he has done helps us believe in what he can do. You have been surrounded by God's love and redeemed from death. You are loved and empowered by the Spirit of God so you can walk in boldness and authority.

God, thank you for the great things you have done in the past by redeeming mankind. Help me to have faith as I remember all you have done.

CREATED

Since the creation of the world God's invisible qualities—his eternal power and divine nature—have been clearly seen, being understood from what has been made, so that people are without excuse.

ROMANS 1:20 NIV

Have you ever marveled at the power of a storm or sat in awe watching the power of the ocean? Perhaps you have been in the mountains and looked out over creation from a high peak ? It fills our hearts with feelings of wonder and praise for the Creator. But when the world can deny what God has made, they can also reject who he ultimately is. We acknowledge the Creator for his good work, and it fills our hearts with worship when we sit and gaze upon his creation.

As you go about your day, look around you at what he has made, from the smallest creature doing its work, to the grandeur of the skies. Be encouraged that not only is God active in his creation, but he is with you as well.

God, thank you for what you have made and how you have made it. Open my understanding of your creation and fill my heart with praise.

NOBLE THOUGHTS

Whatever is true, whatever is honorable, whatever is just, whatever is pure, whatever is pleasing, whatever is commendable, if there is any excellence and if there is anything worthy of praise, think about these things.

PHILIPPIANS 4:8 ESV

By now you are likely of the age that you practice metacognition. It is a big word that means that you have awareness of your own learning and thinking processes. You may also be aware of your habits of thinking. In other words, you are aware of what you habitually think about.

Paul writes in the book of Romans that we are to renew our minds and have control over our thoughts. In the verse above, he encourages us to think noble thoughts and to dwell upon decency, virtue, justice, and purity. Does Paul mean that we need to think about flowers and such? Possibly, but he is encouraging maturity of thought and recognizing what our minds are set upon. We need to be aware that we can change our thinking habits. When our minds are positive, pure, and set on loving God, it changes our countenance and our actions.

Father, help me to dwell upon you. I ask that my thoughts would be your thoughts and my ways become your ways.

MATURITY

Solid food is for the mature, who by constant use have trained themselves
to distinguish good from evil.
HEBREWS 5:14 NIV

There is nothing like going to the local take-out restaurant and getting that favorite menu item. As we wipe our faces with remnants of the last big bite, we boast that we could eat it every day. And it's true. We likely could eat it every day, but what would happen if we did? Doctors tell us all the time that weight, blood, and heart issues are the most common health ailments. It's even likely that eating unhealthy food will lead to early death. So, as we get older, we discern that we need to eat healthier more regularly. In maturity, we discern and practice the way we live differently.

As you grow in Christ, you also learn by training. You learn what the things are that you should avoid in order to be a healthier Christian and a better person. You have within you the Holy Spirit to help you mature in this way. Be confident that he is with you and speaking to you. Listen carefully for his voice.

Holy Spirit, please help me to hear you and to learn the things that you are teaching me. I want to be a mature believer and to know Christ in all areas of my life.

THE NEED TO WAIT

I waited patiently for the LORD;
and He inclined to me, and heard my cry.
PSALM 40:1 NKJV

Have you ever wanted something really badly and yet you had to wait for it? The desire for it seems to get stronger as time goes by, especially if we think about it constantly. One of the hardest things to do is to wait when we really want something. It might even seem impossible. Our desire to "have" is strong and we must learn how to control it. It is the same impulse that Adam and Eve experienced in the garden of Eden at the fall of man. But when Jesus came, he told us to wait on him, to be with him, and to follow him. If you do this, you will remain in him, and he will live in you. Even better, he will never leave you.

Ultimately, you follow Jesus because you know that it is what you want, and it is right. You will learn to be patient and to stop your wants from being met right away as you practice self-control. Self-control leads to patience and waiting. That is something only Jesus can do in you. God listens to those who wait on him. He is ready for you to wait!

Jesus, help me to learn to wait on you and be patient. I want to remain in you forever!

FOR HIS GLORY

Whether you eat or drink, or whatever you do,
do everything for the glory of God.

1 CORINTHIANS 10:31 NRSV

Do everything for God so that it glorifies him. That is a big ask. How does that work when you study, work, eat, or even go to the bathroom? Like, literally everything?! Yes, in a way, we are to do everything for his glory, but it happens through our attitude. Whether it is the most common of acts, or it has a high spiritual context, our desire should be to do all things by his Spirit.

Think of the times you have done something for your parents, but you didn't really want to. They thanked you for doing it, but your attitude stunk. It doesn't really feel very good. God wants us to serve him in easy or in hard things, and to be happy doing it with a good spirit.

God, help me to be pleasing to you in all that I do. Help my attitude and spirit to be favorable in your sight.

DO THE HARD THINGS

Show yourself in all respects to be a model of good works, and in your teaching show integrity, dignity, and sound speech that cannot be condemned, so that an opponent may be put to shame, having nothing evil to say about us.
TITUS 2:7-8 ESV

It is not popular to be righteous. In fact, the opposite is often true. Our society celebrates wicked and lewd behavior. But God calls us to do hard things: to walk in a manner which reflects his thinking and behavior. One of the easiest ways to fail is in how we speak. The mouth says what is in the heart. We can easily measure where our hearts are at by taking notice of what we say. Do we speak to please God or to fit in with our friends? As we repent of things we say and do, God changes our hearts, and we start to speak and act differently.

You will notice changes in yourself as you continue to grow with God. He will make you a godly man, and you will be strengthened by him as you stand up for what he says.

I want to be a righteous man, God. I ask that the words of my mouth and the focus of my heart would please you at all times.

WITH THE FATHER'S LOVE

There is a time to cry and a time to laugh.
There is a time to be sad and a time to dance.
ECCLESIASTES 3:4 NCV

Being aware of others is an important part of being a Christian. There may be times as we grow in our faith that we struggle to realize what others are going through. We may not even care. We just want to chill without all the hassles and hang-ups that other people have.

But Christ was a man of character and compassion; he cared deeply for people. His disciples are called to engage in the same manner. What that looks like is different than the world's way of ignoring others. It means that we are able to share in a person's pain or joy while setting aside our own feelings. We learn to grow in Christ's love as we start to prefer others above ourselves. As a follower of Christ, you are equipped with all that you need to love others as he does. He has filled you with his Spirit who provides the power and the tools to be a person of strong compassion.

Father, help me to be aware of others and to help them in their troubles or rejoice with them in their joys. Fill me with your Spirit and give me the love that you have for all men.

MAJESTIC

The heavens tell of the glory of God;
And their expanse declares the work of His hands.
Day to day pours forth speech,
And night to night reveals knowledge.

PSALM 19:1-2 NASB

Growing up on a remote island is a unique experience. There is little human interference in the activity of the universe except for that which you yourself make. But at night when the sky is clear, the dark canvas of God's creative genius is on full display. Against this stark background he fills the universe with bright and colorful celestial bodies that catch the eye and fill the soul with wonder. What brilliant mind came up with such incredible wonder?

God, our Creator and Father, made it all. When we follow him, we understand how majestic and mystical his creative expertise is. He is worthy of our praise and our intrigue. As you continue reading the Word, fill your heart with wonder and dig deeply into the character and creativity of God. He is amazing, and he wants you to be captivated by who he is.

God, you are incredible, and I am filled with wonder when I dwell upon all you have made. Help me to know you more and to fill my heart with revelations of you.

JOY IN FOLLOWING

May the righteous be glad and rejoice before God;
may they be happy and joyful.
PSALM 68:3 NIV

Living a life that pleases God is difficult. Jesus said it would not be easy. We may have to stand up against people who make fun of us. Even worse is when our friends are choosing something we know is not godly and we say something. Sometimes it even comes to the point where we have to find new friends. If so, Jesus promises a great reward in this life and later when he returns.

You will have joy as you follow him today even if it is difficult. He has made it clear that you will be filled with hope and peace in this life though there may be trouble all around you. His promise is to be with you and to comfort you in all your trouble.

Thank you, Jesus, for sending the Holy Spirit to help me and bring me joy and peace. I need your help to do what is right and to be happy in it.

ABOUT YOU

He knows our frame;
He remembers that we are dust.
PSALM 103:14 NKJV

Have you ever started sharing something with a friend and they start talking about themselves? You kind of feel ripped off; you were sharing, and they just turned it into something about themselves. Now think about a friend who listens and asks you more. They may even reflect what you feel. That is a person who understands. It feels good to talk to a friend like that.

This is the friend that Jesus is to us. In Hebrews chapter four, the Bible says that he is a High Priest who empathizes with our weaknesses. He knows how we are made, and he gets it. He gets us. You have a Savior and a God who knows you. He became human like you, so you know that he completely understands you. Know today that God is with you.

Father, thank you for sending Jesus to become a man and show me how to live in a manner that pleases you. Thank you for understanding me and helping me to become more like you.

UNGODLY DESIRES

I delivered to you as of first importance what I also received: that Christ died for our sins in accordance with the Scriptures, that he was buried, that he was raised on the third day in accordance with the Scriptures.

1 CORINTHIANS 15:3-4 ESV

The gospel of Jesus Christ is simple and yet profound. The storyline of humanity is that we fell away from a relationship with God. Our rebellion and wrongful desire are common to all men. Yet, Christ came and died in our place. He suffered immensely for our sake so that we would not have to. Then he was resurrected into eternal life so that we could also live eternally. Our lives are truly a gift from him. Without his death and resurrection, there would be no need for Christianity. This Scripture makes up the core of what we believe and follow.

Christ died for your sins, and he asks you to die to your desires that lead you away from him. They have no power over you. Trust in him to lead you to do what is right. He has given you the keys to choose and walk with him today.

Father, help me to follow Christ in doing what is right and dying to the desires of my flesh. Give me the strength to walk out my faith and follow Christ.

PRESIDENT CHORES

Since the world began, no ear has heard and no eye has seen a God like you,
who works for those who wait for him!

ISAIAH 64:4 NLT

Can you imagine the president coming to your home and doing your chores for you? Perhaps he turns up and says, "Hey, I just wanted to show you I care about you. You are important." You would be blown away. Doesn't he have better things to do with his time?

Though this is very unlikely, we do serve an amazing God who has done more for us than simple chores. He has given his life for us. And every day, he continues to show us his kindness and care. The Bible says that we can cast our cares upon him because he cares for us. This is the God we serve. You have a God who walks with you. The Holy Spirit is constantly present in your soul and in your life teaching, comforting, and leading you. Listen for his voice and wait to hear what he is saying.

Holy Spirit, thank you for being with me. Thank you for caring for me and showing me how to walk as a believer in Christ.

SOURCE FOR LOVE

Love bears all things, believes all things,
hopes all things, endures all things.
1 CORINTHIANS 13:7 ESV

There is only one source for love like this and it is found in Jesus Christ. As humans, we find it very difficult to bear, believe, hope, and endure all things. Take a moment to dwell upon this and think about the worst thing you may be able to endure. How about a sibling or friend who does that annoying thing over and over again? It doesn't take us long to become irritated and lash out. But Jesus does not become angered like we do. He is patient and kind. He is tough and enduring. He can handle us and our mistakes.

God has given you his love and asks that you would love others similarly. You will not be able to perfect it, but you can learn and grow in it. You are equipped to love others better because of the Spirit of Christ in you.

Father, thank you for giving me all that I need for life and godliness. Help me to lay down my life and serve others today. I want to act like Jesus.

WAKE UP

Commit to the LORD whatever you do,
and he will establish your plans.
PROVERBS 16:3 NIV

There is one way to ensure that your life aligns with God's plan for you. You must commit your ways to him. That looks like waking up and acknowledging him as one of your first steps. It means that you're inviting him to participate in your day and asking him to be present with you. Then, as you go about your day, you will listen and look for him because he is actively with you.

Upon retiring to your bed and after laying down your gadgets and electronics, you will pause and prayerfully reflect upon his presence with you throughout your day. You will ask him to give you the right dreams, and you'll thank him for his greatness and goodness. This will allow your plans to be established and your days to be fruitful for God's kingdom. You are a son of God, and he loves to do things with you. Keep inviting him into your life because he wants to be with you.

Father, thank you for being the perfect Dad. You are always present and attentive. You want to be with me, and I need that reminder throughout my day.

YES AND NO

Each of us should please our neighbors for their good,
to build them up.
ROMANS 15:2 NIV

There is a popular movie about a man who always said no. It didn't matter what it was; he would just say no. It meant he missed out on lots of opportunities in life. He even quoted Jesus' words that we should make sure our no is a firm one. The man is then challenged to say yes which shakes him up a little. No more no. He has to say yes to everything. Life gets crazy for him!

God wouldn't want us to do this either. Saying yes to everything would quickly exhaust us. We cannot please everyone! There is a healthy balance between the two. The most critical part of the decision between yes and no is being committed to what you say you will do and not allowing selfishness to rule your decisions. As you learn how to be pleasing to others, you realize that God is helping you to look beyond yourself to the needs of others. Be encouraged that God is working in you today.

God, I ask that you would help me to be aware of others. Give me your eyes for people and help me to be willing to serve.

EYES FIXED

He said, "Come." So Peter got out of the boat,
started walking on the water, and came toward Jesus.
MATTHEW 14:29 NRSV

We always have an invitation to come to Jesus. We may not be sure of ourselves or where we stand, yet Jesus always asks us to come to him. We may not always meet with him because we are hesitant. Perhaps we only take one step his way. But that isn't enough, just like it wasn't enough with Peter. Shortly after his great steps of faith when he got out of the boat, Peter stopped believing. He looked at his surroundings. He saw the ocean, the wind, and the waves. Suddenly he sank, and he cried out.

The cool end to the story is that Jesus saved him. Even though we may not follow through all the way, and our faith inevitably fails, Jesus comes to rescue us. What a great God we serve! Jesus promises to never leave you or forsake you. He says that though your sins be as scarlet, he can make them white as snow. Never turn away from him because he wants you to come to him.

Jesus, thanks for being such a great support. I need you today to help me keep my eyes fixed on you and you alone.

FLOODED AND FILLED

This light momentary affliction is preparing for us an eternal weight of glory beyond all comparison, as we look not to the things that are seen but to the things that are unseen. For the things that are seen are transient, but the things that are unseen are eternal.

2 CORINTHIANS 4:17-18 ESV

Sometimes it seems as though the whole world is against us. Our parents are getting on us about everything under the sun. Our siblings and friends are annoying. People in general seem to be crabby. It's hard in those times not to become overwhelmed and disappear into ourselves. Yet, Christ calls us to look past these momentary times and see what is unseen. We have access through all the difficult times to his promises, his power, his majesty, and his faithfulness. He continues to be with us though we are surrounded by struggle.

He calls you to lift up your head and look to him. Allow his power and promises to flood your mind and fill your heart with joy. He is all that you need right now, and he calls you to love and serve others (in spite of their stinky attitudes).

Jesus, thank you for your example. Fill my heart with praise in the midst of difficult times, and flood me with love for others like you have for me.

IN THE DAY-TO-DAY

Perfect, absolute peace surrounds those
whose imaginations are consumed with you;
they confidently trust in you.

ISAIAH 26:3 TPT

Jesus gave us great imaginations. As we get older, we may not practice using them like we used to. We are swamped with media which fills us with created content. In countries where children have few possessions, they still come up with creative ways to play. For example, you may see children binding bendy sticks into a ball and hitting it around with bigger sticks. What imaginative things did you come up with recently? We can get really creative when we are bored and need something to entertain us. Part of that creativity is to imagine who God is and what he can do. Think about the earth and how amazing it is; God made it!

As you go about your day, take time to imagine God interacting with you and creation. Be filled with peace, as you remember that he is constantly with you. God's Spirit is present within you.

Holy Spirit, fill me with thoughts of God and help me to see him in my day-to-day activities.

SMALL THINGS

We are his workmanship, created in Christ Jesus for good works,
which God prepared beforehand, that we should walk in them.
EPHESIANS 2:10 ESV

What do we devote our time, money, and talent to? Our answers to that question are a good measure of what is important to us. What we think is important may actually be different than how we live, and if so, we may feel confused and disoriented. Do the things we think are important align with the things we spend our time doing, what we spend our money on, or where we use our talent? If so, we are living with integrity, and we're being true to ourselves.

If what we value and how we live are not aligned, our lives will feel conflicted. There will be an ongoing, unsettled feeling within us. We find alignment with what is central and crucial to us as we seek God. He helps us find the vital thing that we should be doing, and he can put us in the right place to do it. Your life is a journey and God is preparing you for great things. Don't miss or dismiss the little, obedient things you are doing in this moment that prepare you for the key thing you will do later. God is active in you.

Father, help me to obey you in the small things today, so I will be ready for the great things you will do through me.

LIKE YOU LOVE ME

This is how God showed his love to us:
He sent his one and only Son into the world
so that we could have life through him.

1 JOHN 4:9 NCV

Imagine a dad sending his only son away, knowing that he would have to suffer great physical and emotional pain. His friends would abandon him. The blood would run from the lashings on his back as the whip ripped the flesh from his bones. Thorns and a spear would pierce him, and he would cry out for help. The dad, however, had to wait, watch, and do nothing. Eventually the son would die from his wounds.

It seems unbearable to us to let someone suffer like this. Yet God did this in order to show his love for us. He allowed suffering for his most loved Son in order to show the most beautiful love for us. He knew the outcome, however. His Son would overcome death and rise again. What an incredible Father to endure this for the sake of all mankind. You are loved with this same love. God draws you to himself, longs for you to understand his love, and wants you to be fully devoted to him.

Father, thank you for showing me such great love. Jesus, thank you for suffering so greatly to save me. Help me to draw close to you, God, and love others like you love me.

DEVOTED AND FAITHFUL

The Lord is faithful;
he will strengthen you and guard you from the evil one.
2 Thessalonians 3:3 NLT

We love to watch fails. It is hilarious to see a person slip, crash a bike, bounce too high, or belly flop in the water. We can spend hours watching clips like this. But the truth is, we don't like ourselves when we experience failure. We don't want to fail. We love success. We feel our best when we do something right. That is why God is so awesome. He never fails. He finishes all that he starts, and he does well at it. He is faithful.

When God says that he will protect you, and that you will have eternal life, you can be sure that he will do what he says. You do not have to fear anything. He is with you always and will protect your life from the devil. Obey God and follow him with all your heart because he will never leave you or forsake you.

God, I want my life to be devoted to you. Help me to be faithful to you as you are to me.

SELF-CONTROL

The end of all things is at hand; therefore, be self-controlled
and sober-minded for the sake of your prayers.

1 PETER 4:7 ESV

We love Jesus. We want to obey him and follow his ways. He is right, pure, good, and true. Yet it is difficult to say no to our urges and to think things through before we act or speak. We often regret our secret actions that we didn't want to do in the first place. We wanted to honor God, but we failed. However, as we grow in Christ, he teaches us through his Holy Spirit the practice of self-control. We learn to discipline our bodies and our minds. He also helps us to see what is happening in the world and to be mindful of it. He helps us to be thoughtful in our words and our actions.

You have the Holy Spirit in you, and he teaches you every day. He helps you with self-control. Rely upon him, fill your mind with the Word of God, and allow his wisdom to guide you.

Jesus, thank you for the Holy Spirit. Holy Spirit, show me how to live with control, and give me the grace to obey. God, I want to love you more and I want my whole being to follow you.

LOYAL

A friend is always loyal,
and a brother is born to help in time of need.
PROVERBS 17:17 NLT

We are very blessed if we have one: someone who is there when we need help, always around when we want to hang out, or ready to go when we want to do something. For some, it might be a dog. A boy's best friend is incredibly dependable. When you go away, no matter how long it's for, the one who is happiest and most excited to see you is your dog.

Your pup doesn't let up when you get home; he smells all the new smells, catching up on all the places you've been. He wants the whole story, and he follows you around the house until you are sitting down and relaxed. Then he plants himself at your feet, content that you are present. If you are happy, he's happy; if you are upset, he comforts you. If you are angry at him and push him away, he comes back soon afterward. No matter what, your dog does not stop wanting to be with you. That is a dependable friend. As you live for Christ and follow him, you will have a steady friend in the Holy Spirit. He was sent to be your comforter and counselor; he is your truthful, loyal companion.

Holy Spirit, help me to be aware of you in my life and to follow Christ loyally.

GLORY

On the glorious splendor of your majesty,
and on your wondrous works, I will meditate.
PSALM 145:5 NLT

It was hard to fall asleep. They had to be up before dawn and out the door by three-thirty in the morning. It wouldn't exactly be the longest rest, especially when the adrenaline was pumping. But morning came, and they were on the road, excited about what lay ahead. At just a little after four, they parked the car. The starry sky glittered above them, and the chill of the air bit at their exposed skin. Hiking this early in the morning required additional lighting, so they slowly clambered up the rocky face of the mountain with their headlamps lighting the way. From below it looked like fireflies crawling along the ridge, joining the glittering stars.

By the time they crested the peak, the sun was just about to awaken. It had lightened significantly since they started and now, two hours in, sweaty and tired bodies gathered on flat rocks awaiting the splendid display. Everyone's expectations were exceeded as the magnificent colors shifted and changed until the sun broke forth from the horizon. It was a superb morning to be alive.

Jesus, help me to take time to enjoy what you have created and to be filled with praise for what you have made.

NEVER LET DOWN

Those who know your name trust in you,
for you, LORD, have never forsaken those who seek you.
PSALM 9:10 NIV

Have you ever worked hard to earn a position on a team, saved to buy something special, or entered a tough competition… only to be met with disappointment when it didn't happen? It is such a letdown. Your heart fills with sadness and loss. Often you don't even know how to express what you feel or where to turn in your confusion.

God wants us to turn to him and tell him what we feel. He is trustworthy. When we need him to show up, he never fails. We may not always have the eyes to see, but God never lets us down. He has his perfect timing and his loving ways of doing things, so we can trust in him always. As you grow in your relationship with God and as you read his Word, your heart will gain understanding of his ways and how trustworthy he is. You can trust God.

Father, help me understand your ways and trust in your character. You are a faithful God who never disappoints those who seek you.

CLOSER THROUGH CHALLENGES

"No longer do I call you servants, for the servant does not know what his master is doing; but I have called you friends, for all that I have heard from my Father I have made known to you."

JOHN 15:15 ESV

A friend can be closer than a brother, or a brother can be your closest friend. What drives those relationships is our ability to share about ourselves with one another and to allow trust to form even when faced with difficulty. Friendships face strain at times, but the friendship between two people can overcome trouble. It often can grow even closer through those challenges. We find through the challenging times in our healthy friendships, that we are encouraged to mature into good men. Brave friends keep us from complaining about life and help us to recognize bad habits. They help us see how we can find healing and wisdom in God.

Jesus says that he is also your friend. Why would God be your friend? How can you be a friend to God? All he asks of you is to seek him and share your day with him. Try this: start your day with an invitation and end your day with a thank-you to him.

Jesus, I invite you to be a part of my day. Lead me in ways that please you and fill my mind with good, pure, and true thoughts. I commit my day to you.

RECEIVED WITH MERCY

The steadfast love of the LORD never ceases;
his mercies never come to an end;
they are new every morning;
great is your faithfulness.

LAMENTATIONS 3:22-23 ESV

When we sin against God, we have an advocate, a friend that stands before God and who appeals to him for mercy. His name is Jesus, the Son of God who died for our sins and shed his blood on our behalf. Because of this never-ending mercy, we can come to Jesus, thank him for his kindness, and repent of our sins. He forgives us willingly.

In God's kingdom we can wake up every day like it is new, carrying no guilt or sin before God. We can walk in confidence that he loves us and cares for us. He is faithful to love us all the time despite our failures. What an amazing, kind, and great God we serve! As you read and take in his Word, trust that he forgives your confessed sins, and he will never turn you away. Whenever you come to God in humility, he will receive you with mercy.

Thank you, God, for your kindness and deliberate love. Help me to love you in return and to trust you always.

OBEY ONLY GOD

By a single offering he has perfected for all time
those who are being sanctified.
HEBREWS 10:14 ESV

It was a bloody and messy affair. The slaughter of animals for the sin of men was a common practice in the Old Testament. Bulls, sheep, goats, and doves were all offerings for different reasons. This was a regular practice and it reminded Israel of how they had broken the law, that they needed to repent, and against whom they had sinned—God. Since Jesus became our final offering and died on our behalf, we no longer take sacrifices to the temple. However, every day we need to follow Christ, and in many ways, we choose to give up or sacrifice something in order to do so.

You have many opportunities to love things other than God. Yet here you are seeking him, reading his Word, and reflecting on him. You are living for God. Keep doing so by repenting of your sin regularly and humbling yourself before him in prayer.

Father, I want to obey you, and I willingly lay down what I want in order to run after you. Thank you, Jesus, for being my sacrifice. Help me now to let go of the things I want and to follow you.

SHAPED

Now, O Lord, you are our Father;
we are the clay, and you are our potter;
we are all the work of your hand.

Isaiah 64:8 esv

You may be taking a class in pottery. If you have the opportunity, it is a worthwhile course. Basically, you make useful or artistic items out of clay. After shaping a clay creation as you desire, you place it in a hot kiln to harden, which still allows it to be porous enough to absorb a glaze. Glaze allows colors and coatings to be applied so that the pottery is both useful for the home and less fragile as a decorative piece. Then a second kiln bakes the glaze onto the pottery. In the end, you have a creative work from your own hands that you can be proud of and is useful in some fashion.

You are clay in the hands of God, and he is forming you and making you useful for his kingdom. Continue to humbly allow him to form you and make you his own. He is gentle and precise in his work and makes only great pieces of pottery!

Father, I want to be shaped by your hands and not by this world. Help me to humbly follow you and obey your Word. Please speak to me, Holy Spirit, and teach me God's ways.

COMMIT TO THE GOAL

In him we were also chosen, having been predestined according to the plan of him who works out everything in conformity with the purpose of his will, in order that we, who were the first to put our hope in Christ, might be for the praise of his glory.

EPHESIANS 1:11-12 NIV

Jesus planned to save us and completed his task when he suffered, was killed, buried, and then resurrected. He did not pause in pursuing his goal. As a child, he sought out his Father in the temple. As a man, he purposefully suffered to the point of death. Now, as the resurrected Savior, he continues to pray for us. When he finally returns as the warrior King, he will complete his goal by restoring creation to the Godhead. Have you seen a man committed to his goal like Jesus was and still is? He is worthy of our admiration.

As you read the Scripture above, believe that he is working with you for the purpose of his will. Be encouraged that he is actively speaking to you.

Jesus, help me to hear you and to know what you have planned for me. You are making me like you, and I pray that my heart and mind would follow you willingly.

UNSELFISH

Do not merely look out for your own personal interests,
but also for the interests of others.
PHILIPPIANS 2:4 NASB

Humans are designed such that they are inclined to take care of themselves. It starts from that first cry; a quick response from our parents helps us to know that our needs will be taken care of. As we grow, we learn that when we do certain things that make people respond favorably, we do them more. This develops a healthy attachment. When our parents teach us well, we learn that we are a part of a larger system, and that as we contribute, the system runs smoothly. All within it are content. It is in our families that we learn what it means to be considerate, to have concern for others, and to demonstrate understanding. We grow our respect for the needs of others, and in doing so, we become part of the structure that takes care of those needs.

In your family, you have the opportunity to demonstrate Christ's love by being considerate of others. You have Christ in you to help you love like he loves by giving up your needs to serve others.

Jesus, help me to love others as you do. I want to think about others before I get what I want and to love them more than I love myself.

REMEMBER REALLY WELL

Keep this Book of the Law always on your lips; meditate on it day and night,
so that you may be careful to do everything written in it. Then you will be
prosperous and successful.

JOSHUA 1:8 NIV

What are the things you remember really well? Is it the names of your
favorite players and their stats? Perhaps it is the best strategy for a
game, or how to beat an opponent? Is it the words of a song? Maybe it is
subjects you are studying and trying to master? Without even noticing,
we are filling our minds with matter, some of it helpful, some of it useless.
It gets there because we practice it by intentional study, or because we
think and talk about it.

God's Word is important in our faith and requires the same interest
and study as all these other subjects. You have within you the capacity
to focus on God's Word, and to allow it to fill your heart and mind. Be
captivated by it and read it regularly. It will encourage you to follow
Christ.

*Holy Spirit, help me to read the Word and to be filled with hunger for it.
I want to be able to remember it like I remember so many other things.*

AWAY FROM WORLDLY PASSIONS

The grace of God has appeared that offers salvation to all people. It teaches us to say "No" to ungodliness and worldly passions, and to live self-controlled, upright and Godly lives in this present age.

TITUS 2:11-12 NIV

Jesus calls us to live differently than other people in the world. What does that look like? He asks us to not be filled with lust, the love of money, or the pursuit of our own pleasures. These are the worldly passions that we see promoted in the media. Jesus promises eternal life, pleasure, and the enjoyment of his creation forever if we faithfully follow him. He asks us to show love by controlling ourselves and serving others. He wants us to practice righteousness and love justice. These are hard in a life that is filled with messages to pursue pleasure.

God has given you everything you need to love him and follow his commands. He promises so much more than what you can get in this brief life. His eternal pleasures will be given to those who follow him wholeheartedly.

Jesus, I want to follow you and love others well. I ask for your help to live differently than others do; to speak your truth in love, and to walk justly with you.

IN THE HEART

As in water face reflects face,
so the heart of man reflects the man.
PROVERBS 27:19 ESV

What is in the heart of a man? Jesus said it is clear in the words we speak. How do we talk? What do we talk about? Are our words adapted to who we are with? With our Christian friends do we speak "Christianese," using words that please God and the church? Then with our other friends, do we swear, make dirty jokes, or talk about sinful things? If so, our hearts may not yet be sure of who or what to follow.

As we keep seeking God, he helps us mature. He helps us to control our tongues and to have hearts that seek him only. He is kind and faithful to lead us, so that our words and actions reflect his desires. You can trust God to make you into a man who represents him well. He will make your words and the intentions of your heart like his.

Thank you, Jesus, for saving me. Thank you, Father, for giving me everything I need to be like Jesus and to follow after him. I ask for your help to keep following Christ.

TESTIMONY

Be wise in the way you act toward outsiders; make the most of every opportunity. Let your conversation be always full of grace, seasoned with salt, so that you may know how to answer everyone.

COLOSSIANS 4:5-6 NIV

In our adolescence it is really important for us to have good friends. We are strongly influenced in behavior and speech by those we hang out with. This can be helpful for our faith, or it can influence us negatively. It all depends on our friends. It is important that we choose friends who encourage our faith in Christ. Not only is it good for us, but it is also important for our testimony about who Christ is.

When we are built up in our faith, we are encouraged to speak and to act in ways that exemplify Jesus. When we do, it helps those who do not know him see what he is like. You can make a difference in how Christ is seen by people who do not know him. As you walk and talk today, be aware of your language and actions. Bring Jesus glory in all that you do.

Jesus, help me to be a good witness of your character and of who you are. I want to be like you.

JESUS KNOWS

To him who is able to do immeasurably more than all we ask or imagine,
according to his power that is at work within us.
EPHESIANS 3:20 NIV

Being given the captaincy of a sports team is an honor. Sometimes coaches pick the least expected player for such roles and when they do, teammates may wonder why. What is it about that player that made him good enough to be captain? Empowering someone is not always about recognizing the leadership that is already evident; rather, it is about seeing in a player the attributes that could make a great leader. After all, leaders are made, not born.

A good coach can see what a team needs and then equip people on the team who are capable of fulfilling those needs. Often teams have more than one captain. Some lead because of their attributes, and some are empowered to lead because a coach sees future abilities and wants to encourage them. Jesus is even more knowledgeable about what you need and how to empower you. He sees great potential in you and doesn't shame you into action. He calls you into it by empowering you with the Holy Spirit.

Holy Spirit, help me today to understand Jesus more and to trust him to lead me in all areas of my life.

REWARDS

> "Blessed are the meek,
> for they shall inherit the earth."
> MATTHEW 5:5 ESV

Is meek weak? Must the meek turn their cheek? The way of Jesus was not seen as weak. It was strong, upright, and true. The Holy Spirit spoke through Jesus words of truth and life that pierced the darkness and destroyed strongholds. So even though he did not fight physically, he did not lash out at others mentally, and he appeared gentle and lowly, he was not quiet when it suited God's purposes. This is the key.

We sometimes live in fear that our own pride will be done in, so we fight for it. We might say that we don't deserve to be treated certain ways, and we may even be right in those circumstances. But does our fighting suit God's purposes or are we serving our own? You will be rewarded when you follow God's ways and not your own. He said the meek will inherit the earth, not the ones concerned about their own reputation and pride. As you go about your tasks today, remember that God is your reward, and you cannot reward yourself. He is your true source of life.

God, I ask that you would help my mind to be set on your rewards and not on my pride or what I want. You are all that I need.

CHOICES

"If you refuse to serve the LORD,
then choose today whom you will serve.
But as for me and my family, we will serve the LORD."

JOSHUA 24:15 NLT

There is something inspirational about a decisive person; they actively and confidently make decisions and take ownership of their responsibilities. Who would not like to be this way? The foolish make rash choices and are reactionary in their responses. The Bible makes it clear that their doom will come quickly. The impulsive man does not think before he reacts. The decisive man considers his way and acts.

Your decisions can be paralyzed by fear of failure. You may compare yourself with others or worry about what has not occurred. These fears and doubts are relieved when you surrender your decisions to Christ and recognize that your hope lays in him and in his final word over you. Ultimately, you serve God, and your choices are committed to him as you walk in obedience to his voice.

Jesus, I trust in you to help me make good decisions. I choose to serve you today.

CREATION

"Be still, and know that I am God.
I will be exalted among the nations,
I will be exalted in the earth!"
PSALM 46:10 ESV

The mountains were high above him, capped with black cliffs that were frosted by white snow. The sun was bright, the sky was blue, and their reflections created imaginary sapphires shimmering in the stream. Birds chirped in the green canopy above while squirrels tussled in the leaves below. He loved these moments of tranquility with no one around: just nature at its best and the Creator by his side. He found in these times that stillness returned to his soul. The worries of life drifted away, and he found a soothing rhythm in the relaxing sounds that pleased his ears.

You can find great peace in God's creation. When you take a break from the media-filled life most of us experience, and enter into the stillness of God's rest, you will find calm in your soul. Take time to go out in creation and find your rest in him.

You are amazing, God! Thank you for your creation. Help me to connect with you as I praise and thank you for what you have made.

A GOOD FOLLOWER

If children, then heirs, heirs of God and joint heirs with Christ—
if, in fact, we suffer with him so that we may also be glorified with him.
ROMANS 8:17 NRSV

When a person dies and there is not a living relative to claim the inheritance or the state cannot find one, the inheritance goes to the state. Currently some states have over two billion dollars in unclaimed funds! That seems like a great deal of work and wealth stored up for nothing. It's kind of like playing a game for hours, even days, on your console. You have won a ton of rewards, spent hundreds on upgrades, skins, and items, and then you lose your account. Everything is gone in one instant. Tons of work is just lost to nothingness. How much better would it have been if you could have given it to someone? Or even better, wouldn't it have been nice if you could have kept it forever?

God also has a great wealth. He has stored it up for you to keep forever. As you go about your day, be reminded that God is preparing you to receive a great inheritance. Jesus worked hard to provide us a way for this to happen. You are an heir of a much greater reward than anything this life can give.

Jesus, help me to not squander what you have prepared for me. I want to be a good follower who brings you glory.

SIMPLY SERVE

"The greatest among you shall be your servant.
Whoever exalts himself will be humbled,
and whoever humbles himself will be exalted."
MATTHEW 23:11-12 ESV

Of all the things a man can do to humble himself, understanding the meaning of the word serve must be at the core. A servant simply serves others, doing menial tasks. In our wonderfully liberated society, as you get older and become a man, no one owns you but you, yourself. You can start or quit working when you want. You can start and own a business at a young age, or you can just work for a company. You have the freedom to choose.

To serve others intentionally is an act of humility that pleases God. This is the will of God. You may not be there yet, but you can start with your family. Pick up after your siblings, clean the kitchen, or bring someone a drink. Simple service is pleasing to God.

God, I want to learn how to serve others and care about them. Help me to practice being a servant. Help me to love others like you do.

LISTEN FOR HIS VOICE

I waited patiently for the LORD;
and He inclined to me, and heard my cry.
PSALM 40:1 NKJV

How easy is it to wait? When you know what you want and are ready for it to happen, what is your patience level like? For most of us, it is difficult. When we have something on our mind and it is accessible enough, we go after it. But should we always? What about pausing to wait and ask God first? Being able to wait before taking is something we learn early in life. It starts in infancy when our parents teach us. As we grow, we start to practice it ourselves and it leads us to self-control, which is a fruit of the Spirit.

The Holy Spirit dwells in you to provide patience and self-control, not just for your own benefit, but so you can wait on God and have him show up to do great things in you. Run, but don't run ahead of him. Patiently listen for his voice and allow him to speak to you today.

Father, help me to hear the Holy Spirit and obey his voice. I want you to help me be patient and self-controlled.

VALID

Now we see only a reflection as in a mirror; then we shall see face to face.
Now I know in part; then I shall know fully, even as I am fully known.
1 CORINTHIANS 13:12 NIV

There is a desire that drives much of what we do: to be truly known and accepted. Our common focus is often to achieve; we want to build friendships, wealth, find security, receive accolades, and grow our empires. The bigger and greater that is, the better we feel about ourselves. Even if we don't find success in these things, we still desire them, believing they will validate us and make us more powerful or likeable. We also want relationships, but those are often treated as secondary to other goals. God, however, made us for relationships. He said right at the outset that it is not good for us to be alone. His focus is not on what we accomplish, but on our relationships.

You will find joy and satisfaction when you realize and accept that your validation comes from being known just as you are without any string of achievements. God does this. He validates you because you are his son, not because of what you have done.

God, I am your child. Though I may not always see it in myself, or reflect you in my behavior, help me to believe that you are my Father, and I am your child.

FELLOWSHIP

All Scripture is inspired by God and is useful for teaching,
for showing people what is wrong in their lives, for correcting faults,
and for teaching how to live right.

2 TIMOTHY 3:16 NCV

Some would say that the Bible is no longer relevant. It's true that the Bible does not hold answers for *every* situation in life. We also find that God has revealed truths throughout creation and within different cultures. However, the Bible is critical and applicable in so many ways, none more so than when we pray with the Word and listen to the Holy Spirit. It is in this place that we find answers to life's questions.

Additionally, and critical to our faith, is the fellowship we find with other believers. Our hearts are deceitful, and we can be led astray even when we study the Word regularly. Our buffer for our own deception is found within committed relationships to a body of people who pursue Christ. Try to regularly join with other believers and study the Word or pray together. Today, reach out to friends who have a strong faith and encourage them with a Bible verse.

Jesus, help me to be with friends who love you, and give me words to encourage them in their faith.

TOGETHER IN FAITH

Encourage each other and give each other strength,
just as you are doing now.
1 THESSALONIANS 5:11 NCV

Have you ever tried to move a large boulder or a tree trunk by yourself? Perhaps you have helped someone move and tried to pick up an item that was heavier than you thought it would be. To get it done, you have to have help. You need the strength of another person. Jesus teaches that we need relationships. In particular, we need to be with people of faith.

Consider this: if you want to encourage someone in science, mechanics, or research, you can't just say, "You are doing a good job," without understanding what they do. To really encourage someone and to strengthen them, you have to know how to speak into their situation. This is why Christ says that we need to be together in faith. We need to be in the Word in order to understand him and each other as his followers. You have the ability to give strength to your friends and to inspire them in Christ. Call a friend of yours and pray with them or give them some encouragement today.

Jesus, I want to encourage my friends to love you more. Help me to have the right words to say.

SPEAK TRUTH IN LOVE

"I am the way, the truth, and the life.
No one can come to the Father except through me."
JOHN 14:6 NLT

This bold declaration makes it clear that there is no way to have a relationship with God except through Christ. There are many people who teach multiple ways to God, but they are wrong. There is only one way to be without fault before God. This requires us to acknowledge our sin, to repent of it, to recognize Christ as the one who suffered and died for our sin, and to follow his ways. There is no one else who has done this. Jesus is the way, the truth, and the life.

You have a tough decision to make as a disciple of Christ. Many will declare that there are other ways and other gods. You have to decide if you are going to speak the truth or live in agreement with them. God has equipped you to be strengthened to speak the truth with love and gentleness. Jesus is the only way. He speaks the truth, and he is the only one who brings life.

Jesus, help me to share your Word and to love others well while speaking the truth.

IMMEDIATE ACCESS

Our citizenship is in heaven.
And we eagerly await a Savior from there,
the Lord Jesus Christ.
PHILIPPIANS 3:20 NIV

When we are born, we gain immediate access to all the benefits of the country we are born into: a home, family, infrastructure, business, and government. We inherit all of it automatically. We don't earn it or do anything to justify our situation but are simply born into it. That is already an amazing gift to us. We should be grateful. Many people around the world inherit much more difficult situations; their births give them poverty, a shack or a tent, war or devastation; some even die alone.

One bright spot in this broken world is that we all, rich or poor, have the opportunity to inherit something much greater— the promises of Christ. As followers of Christ, we inherit resurrection, life everlasting, a new heaven and earth, and closeness to God forever. You have been re-born in Christ. Just as your birth gave you rights to your country, so your birth in Christ gives you rights to an amazing inheritance.

God, thank you so much for all that I have. Help me to be grateful. I also thank you for all the promises I have in you and the rich inheritance I will receive when you return.

OVERFLOW

"Overflow with mercy and compassion for others,
just as your heavenly Father overflows with mercy and compassion for all."
Luke 6:36 TPT

When we pour a cup of juice, we stop once it reaches the top. God doesn't stop. He just keeps pouring. That is what it means when the Bible says that he overflows with love, forgiveness, and blessings. We know we make mistakes every day. Our thoughts and actions are not as pure as we would like them to be. We all need God to overflow with mercy and compassion. He isn't always angry and ready to punish, watching for our next mistake.

So, too, Jesus asks us to overflow toward one another. Family, friends, and enemies all do things that bug us and hurt us. Yet, just as God continues to be merciful and gracious, he asks us to do the same for others. If you are holding on to grudges and hurts, acknowledge them before God. Tell him how much they hurt, and then ask him to help you forgive the ones who hurt you. Ask him to help you overflow with mercy and compassion.

God, I am angry that people hurt me. I am upset that they do things against me. Yet, as you have forgiven me, help me to forgive them. Thank you for your mercy and compassion.

FOLLOW ME

"My sheep hear my voice, and I know them,
and they follow me."
JOHN 10:27 ESV

Sheep follow. When Jesus talked about his sheep hearing and following his voice, he specifically meant that his sheep would know his voice and come toward their shepherd or follow him to food. They also trust the shepherd to lead them away from danger and to keep them safe. They like to stick together for safety, and they find comfort in numbers. These are a few simple examples of how we are like sheep; we need food, safety, and the comfort of relationships. Jesus is the shepherd who provides all of these for us.

Your relationship with Christ is not meant to be isolated. It is connected to others who also have a relationship with him. That is why he says you need your Christ-following friends, and he encourages you to follow him with them.

Jesus, help me to find friends who love you and want to follow you. I ask that you would protect me from the wolves of the world who want to take me away from following you.

AWE

Be in awe before his majesty.
Be in awe before such power and might!
Come worship wonderful Yahweh, arrayed in all his splendor,
bowing in worship as he appears in the beauty of holiness.
Give him the honor due his name.

PSALM 29:2 TPT

When we take time to plan our actions in detail; when we know what we are going to do after school and what steps we are going to take to accomplish a task, we have complete focus. We could say we are captivated by what we want to do. Perhaps it is meeting up with friends, playing a video game, or attending a sporting activity. Whatever has taken our imagination and interest during the day is likely a passion of ours. This is when we know we are dedicated to something.

Jesus longs for you to be in awe of the things of his kingdom. He wants you to go deeply into the treasure that he has stored up for you. If you listen carefully, he tells you that all these wonderful things you pursue on earth are but a glimpse of what he has in store for you in eternity.

God, help me to be in awe of you and your creation. I want to know your ways and thoughts, and I want to know how to glorify you.

REJOICE

This is the day that the LORD has made;
Let us rejoice and be glad in it.
PSALM 118:24 ESV

You didn't want to get up, but school was happening. You didn't want to do homework, but bad grades are no good. Your friends bailed on something you were looking forward to. Some days stink. We just want them to be over. However, if we can take those bad days and learn from them, they can be really helpful to us. We can find a lot of growth in bad days. Usually, a bad day has some lesson with it, and we can be sure that God is speaking to us regardless of how we feel. He is actively helping us to know him and to become closer to him whether it is a good day or a rough day.

You can rejoice in knowing that God is with you always. Be encouraged to talk to him about your day and be pleased that he is near you. He promises to comfort the brokenhearted and the humble. Come to him and let him know how much you need him.

Father, I need you to comfort me on my bad days. I also want to learn to grow through them. Help me to see with your eyes and not be overwhelmed by my fear, sadness, or grief.

PARTY ON

> Every good gift and every perfect gift is from above, coming down from the Father of lights, with whom there is no variation or shadow due to change.
>
> JAMES 1:17 ESV

We are blessed. It takes time to appreciate this. So often our minds are cluttered with reminders of what we don't have and comparisons with what others do have. But if we can pause a moment, we will realize that we are very fortunate. Why can we confidently say we are blessed? It is not because of what we have or who we live with. It is found in our security in Christ. We have the Holy Spirit in us who is our promise of resurrection into everlasting life. It's not just the promise into any life, but to a restored earth and garden-of-Eden-with-God kind of life. It's far beyond what we can see or imagine.

Think of the times when your parents have taken you home from awesome parties. You wanted to stay and be with your friends forever. Imagine that— fun, friendship, and awesomeness going on forever. This is our promise. Jesus is coming back, and the party will not stop!

God, help me to remember that you are returning and will make all things right. The party will not stop. You do give good gifts and I need help to trust in you.

STEADFAST AND STABLE

Jesus Christ is the same yesterday
and today, and forever.
HEBREWS 13:8 NASB

There is a photo of a man standing outside a lighthouse in front of the entrance. Behind him, a giant wave crashes into the tower; water sprays out as the surge collapses around him. He remains steadfast. Not even the mighty wave moves him. He looks at the camera lens with a firm peace, knowing that he is secure. It is an intriguing photo.

Our lives can be chaotic. We can be the person on the other side of the picture swallowed up by the wave, tumbling and drowning in the disaster. Yet this photo reminds us that somewhere between chaos and order, in the middle of it all and holding it together, is our mighty God. He stands still. He is constant and unbroken by change. He remains stable like the man in the photo. You can be confident that God will remain constant. His character is good and right, and he will always be true to you. You can lean on him and trust him because he cares for you.

I want to trust in you, God. Because of this trust, I want my life to be steadfast and stable even when there is trouble. Help me to believe in you.

HARDWORKING

The slacker wants it all and ends up with nothing,
but the hard worker ends up with all that he longed for.
PROVERBS 13:4 TPT

He was determined to make it work. Stubbornly persevering, he worked day after day. His life was in God's hands, and he knew it, but he also knew that God had given him the gift of tenacity, so he did not stop. Slowly but surely, he saw results, as customer after customer told each other. Word got out about his unwavering commitment; he was service oriented and purposeful. He started with a lawn mower and a secondhand truck, and he went on to grow a multimillion-dollar corporation providing services to thousands of customers.

God didn't create you to be idle. If you have nothing to do but entertainment, you must challenge yourself to up your game. You must be strong in actively pursuing God and serving others. He promises to bless those who are diligent and productive. Today, find a new thing to do that results in others being blessed.

God, help me to turn away from looking for entertainment. I want to be productive for myself and for you. Help me to be a hard worker.

A MIGHTY ONE

The LORD your God is in your midst,
a mighty one who will save;
he will rejoice over you with gladness;
he will quiet you by his love;
he will exult over you with loud singing.

ZEPHANIAH 3:17 ESV

God really does care about us. He does not require much of us either. But number one on his list is really hard—humility. Humility allows us to recognize our true situation; none of us are without sin and sin needs to be paid for. Without humility, this is hard to do. Once we truly understand the need for humility within ourselves, God only asks that we turn to him and ask him for help. When we do, he is ready with a mighty ability to rescue us. He loves to rescue and celebrate us.

Today, cry out to God and he will help you. He loves and rejoices over you. You have no need to fear his rejection. Practice humility and keep short accounts with him. He will always be there for you.

God, thank you for how you love me. Help me to turn my heart to you and keep short accounts with you.

OPTIMISTS ARE MORE FUN

Rejoice in hope,
be patient in tribulation,
be constant in prayer.
ROMANS 12:12 ESV

"It looks like the weather is going to be bad."

"Man, I hate my job."

"This place is boring."

Who likes to chill with Negative Nellie? Few people. Optimists are much more fun. They are cheerful, confident, expectant, and positive; they are enjoyable to be with. Men of faith are optimistic about their futures. They have a hope that is undeniable, possibly in the recesses of their minds, but they know it to be true.

We are clear on this: Christ is returning and will destroy Satan and his followers. He will restore the earth and we will dwell with him on it for eternity. You are called to exude the hope of Christ which is the resurrection of the dead into everlasting life. Be thankful in prayer for what God has done for you.

Father, I want to share this hope that I have within me. I pray for your help to share. I also ask that you would help me to remember your promises and to be thankful.

NO CONFIDENCE IN FLESH

Brothers and sisters, I do not consider myself yet to have taken hold of it.
But one thing I do: Forgetting what is behind and straining toward what is
ahead, I press on toward the goal to win the prize for which God has called me
heavenward in Christ Jesus.

PHILIPPIANS 3:12-14 NIV

Paul writes before this verse that he places no confidence in his flesh.
He had the right to be self-confident because he was faultless according
to the law. He was an upstanding Pharisee who persecuted the church,
and he was a great Hebrew. But he was lost in himself and in his own
confidence. Christ came and set him straight. His resulting repentance
led him to pursue Jesus and to receive his ultimate reward—the
resurrection of his body into life everlasting.

Wherever you are in your faith, you can also be enthusiastic about
seeking him. Talk to God about your past, repent of it, let it go, and see
how he moves you forward. He is faithful.

*God, I know that I have a lot of growing to do. I want to be like Paul, not
assuming that I have made it but always pushing to learn from you and
eventually be rewarded by you.*

HOLINESS

The LORD of hosts is exalted in justice,
and the Holy God shows himself holy in righteousness.
ISAIAH 5:16 ESV

Have you considered the holiness of God? It is hard to imagine what it looks like. According to the Bible, it's something like this: perfect purity, dynamic love, awesome power, all-seeing-eyes, and exacting justice. These powerful descriptions don't even touch how it would feel to stand before a being like this. What would we do? Likely we would fall flat on our faces and weep for mercy. All of our sin, our deepest darkest thoughts, our lack, would be laid bare. There is no chance to explain anything we have done because he would see it all. *Whoa.* That would be an experience no one would forget.

One day, we will all stand before him like this, and we must be ready. God is holy. His is not to be messed with. Yet, because of Christ, he is full of mercy and compassion. He loves beyond your comprehension, and you can approach his holiness with confidence. Because of Christ, you are ready.

Jesus, thank you for making a way for me to approach the holiness of God. I would have no chance otherwise. I love what you have done for me. I repent of my sin and thank you for your forgiveness.

BLESSING OF ENJOYMENT

The LORD is all I need.
He takes care of me.
My share in life has been pleasant;
my part has been beautiful.
PSALM 16:5-6 NCV

He excitedly jumped into the back of the truck that was loaded up with other surfers. He was looking forward to the day ahead. He and his friends joked and laughed as they traversed over the windy roads. Glimpses of the surf break created smiles and a few raised eyebrows. Rounding the bend, the truck skidded to a halt and an awed hush commenced. Perfect waves crested and peeled off along the break. The silence was shattered with shouts of joy and bangs on the truck to get the driver going. The vehicle gunned its engine, gravel peppered the brush behind, and they were away, soon to be enveloped in the ocean's energy.

Hours later, exhausted from squeezing out every last ounce of vigor, the lads sat in silence as the sun set over the ocean. Bright colors splashed across the cirrus clouds that drifted slowly by. His anticipation of the day was fully met; the young man's enjoyment was complete.

God, help me to enjoy what you have created. I want to comprehend your care of me in whatever situation I am in. Help me to trust in the goodness of who you are. You are all I need.

STRENGTH TO BE BRAVE

Overhearing what they said, Jesus told him,
"Don't be afraid; just believe."
MARK 5:36 NIV

The Bible is full of references to God's people being told, " Don't be afraid," or "Be brave." Both speak to a core human emotion —fear. Fear can paralyze us. God knows that we need encouragement to stop being fearful and the strength to be brave. He promised in these references to help us. Jesus, in this verse, claimed that he would do astounding things; the disciples had no need to fear. Shortly after making this statement, he raised a girl to life.

Of all the things we fear, death is one of the greatest, but Jesus overcame death and its finality when he was raised from the dead. Now we do not need to fear anything any longer because we believe! You have the power of the resurrected Christ in you through the Holy Spirit. He is your promise of resurrection and life everlasting. Let this truth fill your heart with confidence and give you boldness to be brave and fearless.

Jesus, thank you for your resurrection power that is within me. Holy Spirit, give me confidence to walk bravely in the promises that you have for me.

REFUGE

You are my hiding place;
You shall preserve me from trouble;
You shall surround me with songs of deliverance.
PSALM 32:7 NKJV

God truly is a place of refuge. He promises to comfort those who turn to him. He is a very real presence in the face of trouble and adversity. How can he do this with so many who cry out to him? The Spirit of Christ dwells with every believer and fills us with the strengthening presence of God when we need it. We still face difficulty in life; he does not promise to remove that from us, but he does guarantee peace.

Because of our future hope in the resurrection, we will have ultimate peace and joy. All of our tears, fears, and pains will be gone. You have the Spirit of Christ in you. Know that today, whether it be a good one or a bad one, Jesus is with you. He wants you to walk and talk with him.

Holy Spirt, I know you are with me. Jesus, thank you for your strength today. Help me to listen for your voice.

AN ENDURING RELATIONSHIP

"O LORD God of heaven, the great and awesome God who keeps covenant
and steadfast love with those who love him and keep his commandments."

NEHEMIAH 1:5 NRSV

God does not change how he faithfully deals with us. His love is
enduring. He also promises consistency and will not mutate into some
weird angry being. His character is steady. We can trust in him. But
notice the dependent clause in this verse, "with those who love him and
keep his commandments." God is faithful, but it is for those who love and
obey him. Who can do this consistently? None. We are dependent on
Jesus. He saves us in our times of failure, and because of who he is, we are
able to have a relationship with the great and awesome God of heaven!

It is good for you to want to please God and to mature in your faith. Keep
doing this and seek out those who live similarly. But when you fail, and
you will, keep short accounts with the awesome God of heaven, through
his Son, Jesus Christ.

*Father, thank you for your Son, Jesus, who has taken away my sins and
allows me to have an enduring relationship with you.*

WHAT IS GOOD

Love must be sincere.
Hate what is evil;
cling to what is good.
ROMANS 12:9 NIV

Our society has collapsed sexually. Sex outside of marriage is common, divorce is rampant, and people across the globe celebrate perverted behavior. Pornography and sex slavery are increasing. Millions of women and children are being sold and imprisoned for others' pleasure. As young men, we are being groomed to feed our lust on a multiplicity of devices. Nothing is inaccessible anymore. It is horrendous in God's eyes. God forgive us and have mercy on us.

You were created as a man to be joined together with a woman, and to one woman only. He wants you to mate for life. You are not an animal, but society wants you to act that way. Be the difference. Learn what it means to prefer one another and to honor each other in love.

Jesus, you didn't make us to live like animals. Thank you for creating healthy sexuality within marriage. I ask that you would help me to learn the difference between love and lust. Give me strength for the former and forgiveness for the latter.

RECONNECTING

Jesus looked at them and said,
"With man this is impossible,
but with God all things are possible."
MATTHEW 19:26 NIV

God never wants relationships to be broken. He calls us to be relationship menders, not relationship breakers. He wants us, as far as it is possible, to be at peace with all men. And he tells us to be reconcilers just as he is, reconnecting people with their broken relationships. He asks us to do this even when it seems impossible.

Jesus spoke truthfully when he said that nothing is impossible with God. God may not always do the things we want, but nothing is out of his ability. He can turn what seems like the worst relationship into something beautiful. In your family, friendships, and church, pray for God to restore relationships. Ask for him to do the impossible and find out how he can use you to help bring healing to others.

Father, teach me to reconnect people like you do. I want to help bring your healing to the hearts of those around me.

EXERCISE

Physical training is of some value, but godliness has value for all things, holding promise for both the present life and the life to come.

1 TIMOTHY 4:8 NIV

When you admire that guy with the well-toned body and think, *It would be great to look like that,* or the athlete who is fit and skilled in his position, *I wish I could be like him,* the question you have to ask yourself is if you want to put in the amount of effort in order to get to where they are. All of a sudden, the desire goes away, and it is replaced with respect. He is doing something you'll likely never do, and it takes lots of work.

When it comes to exercise and healthy eating, you want to do the right thing, but you also fight genetics. A good balance is necessary and less comparison to others is critical. Your health is to be focused on godliness first, which does last into eternity. It does not mean you disregard all else, but you want to keep your focus on what matters most, which is your connection to God.

I thank you, God, for activity and exercise. You made my body well. Help me to look after it and treat it properly. I continue to pray that you help me to grow spiritually. I want to be closer to you.

GREATEST DESIRE

My soul waits in hope for the Lord
More than the watchmen for the morning;
Yes, more than the watchmen for the morning.
PSALM 130:6 NASB

As the sun rose, his eyes adjusted to the brightening landscape. The watchman had been here since midnight, the cold air helping to keep him awake. His legs were tired, and the standing shuffle was the only way to keep his blood flowing while being on guard. He was so thankful it was morning. Sometimes the night was too quiet, and this was one of those watches. Daytime was finally here, and now he could get some food and rest.

You may have times when you were up all night, hanging out with friends and indulging in food and entertainment. In those circumstances, you may not want tomorrow to come early, but the watchman cannot wait. He hungers for the morning. Be hungry for God to show up as you wait upon him.

God, help me to wait patiently for you. I don't want my life to be filled up with other things. I want you to be my greatest desire.

OUTCOME OF SURRENDER

"Don't worry or surrender to your fear.
For you've believed in God, now trust and believe in me also."
JOHN 14:1 TPT

What is the outcome of surrender? Think of history and what that meant for a person or a country. What about some of the games you played when you or your team had given up? Surrender means that you are beaten: that you are subject to the winner. To the victor go the spoils. But what do the surrendered get? They only have defeat.

Worry and fear are no match for Jesus. He overcame them with his death and resurrection. His promises give hope and life. You are not subject to the effects of worry or fear. You can have confidence in Christ, and you can have everlasting life. Be bold and courageous today as you go out into the world.

Jesus, thank you for overcoming the world and setting me free to be full of confidence and life. I need your reminders today that you have saved me, and I am hidden in you. Death and fear cannot touch me.

ADOPTION TAKES SACRIFICE

You have not received a spirit that makes you fearful slaves.
Instead, you received God's Spirit when he adopted you as his own children.
Now we call him, Abba, Father.

ROMANS 8:15 NLT

Accepting a child who is not your own and making a claim that they belong to your family and are your responsibility is a massive commitment. It is also an incredible act of love. Apart from giving your life for someone, adoption may be the most self-sacrificing act a human can make. It is not a new concept to us as it has been practiced throughout history, and there are several examples in the Bible. For instance, God adopted the Israelites as his people. This act eventually led to all of mankind being grafted into his family. What an amazing God of love we serve!

You have the same capacity within you to sacrificially love others. It is the Spirit of Christ that allows you to do so. Your choice to surrender and to live in a manner that pleases him will demonstrate God's love.

God, I want to learn to love like you do. Help me to be willing to sacrifice my wants and allow others to be blessed by my actions. Teach me to be giving and generous like you are.

APRIL 4

ABUNDANCE

They feast on the abundance of your house;
you give them drink from your river of delights.
PSALM 36:8 NIV

Abundant means overflowing, ample, or rich: tons and tons of delights! There is only one who is able to completely fulfill the meaning of this word. God the Father has an endless quantity of supplies to meet all our needs. What is intriguing is that he does not need storehouses for his abundance, for he created all things and can do so with a single word uttered from his mouth. He can create abundance from nothing.

Imagine if your friend had an unlimited supply of everything you needed. Would it be troublesome for him to share with you? What if you were the friend who had everything and could create more at any time? What if you had a limitless ability to meet others' needs? What would your generosity and desire to give be like? Hopefully, you would willingly give out of your abundance. That is what God does for you. If you could even give out of what you don't have, you would see that God will make up the difference.

Help me to trust you, God, and please use me abundantly to bless others. You have all that I need, and I want all that you have for me.

UNRUFFLED BY CIRCUMSTANCES

"May I find favor in your eyes, my lord," she said.
"You have put me at ease by speaking kindly to your servant."
RUTH 2:13 NIV

It should be hard to find a grumpy Christian. How do they even exist? But they do. Sure, we can have bad days or seasons when life gets us down; every human goes through tough times. But a witness of Christ should not represent themselves as consistently sullen or cranky. Why? Because we have received God's promises and a Savior who bore our punishment.

We are to be thankful people. We should have a deep joy, unruffled by circumstances. It was how Paul was able to write about being content in all circumstances. And Jesus, while he walked on earth, was a good-natured man. He was friendly, social, and amicable. You are also called to be a person of peace. As you go about your day, put others at ease, and speak kindly to them. Show them the joy of knowing Christ and be filled with his Spirit.

Holy Spirit, help me to bear the fruit that you promise in Scripture. I want to be filled with kindness, patience, goodness, and self-control. I want joy to fill my heart.

HIS FRUIT IN YOUR LIFE

The LORD will work out his plans for my life—
for your faithful love, O LORD, endures forever.
Don't abandon me, for you made me.
PSALM 138:8 NLT

Sometimes we are discouraged by what is happening in our lives. We may not even know it, so we go on autopilot. We wake up, do school, come home, play video games, do some homework, and go to bed. Then we do the same things over again the next day, and the next, and so on. It's called monotony when the dullness of life takes over.

Jesus came to give us abundant life, and he put in us his Spirit who is full of joy and promise. He desires for us to be connected to the Holy Spirit so that we are encouraged and joyful even when life is monotonous. He has plans for our lives. You can connect and receive from the Spirit of Christ because he dwells within you. His joy is for you. His fruit is in you. Today, join with him and be filled by him.

Holy Spirit, fill me with your joy. I want to live connected to you and be aware of your presence. Help me to know what your plan is for my life.

CREATIVE

God said, "Let us make man in our image, after our likeness.
And let them have dominion over the fish of the sea
and over the birds of the heavens and over the livestock and over all the earth
and over every creeping thing that creeps on the earth."
GENESIS 1:26 ESV

It is amazing that God made us to be like him. The first thing that God did was create. He made us, the heavens and the earth, animals, trees, and plants. As we are made in his image, one of our primary jobs is to create. We were made to make things and to use our imaginations. On this earth there are new things for us to do, things that we have never done before and God says, "Yes, do it! I made you to create."

You have within you creative ideas and concepts that may have sat idle for a long time. If you are too busy with things that others have created (like media, for instance), take time to stop doing those things, and do something new, something from within you.

Father, help me to explore my creativity and not be consumed by this world. I want to see what you can do through me.

NOT IDLE

"This is to my Father's glory,
that you bear much fruit,
showing yourselves to be my disciples."
JOHN 15:8 NIV

If we are to be called Christians, which means little Christs or followers of Christ, we are to do things that he did. Christians are not idle people. They are actively pursuing the things of God and are mindful of what he is doing on the earth. We need to encourage each other to do these things, so that we do not become conformed to this world. It is really easy to go to school or work and then spend the rest of our time being entertained. Jesus asks us to bear fruit and not to be stuck doing what the rest of the world does.

Bearing fruit may be as simple as you serving your family or a neighbor; mow the lawn, rake leaves, do dishes, or clear snow from the driveway. Jesus is not asking you to save the world. Just start with small acts of kindness.

Jesus, help me to bear fruit like you did. I know I can be caught up in what this world offers, but I want to follow you. Help me do that so that I am pleasing to you.

SUBJECT TO HIM

The words "it was credited to him" were written not for him alone, but also for us, to whom God will credit righteousness—for us who believe in him who raised Jesus our Lord from the dead. He was delivered over to death for our sins and was raised to life for our justification.

ROMANS 4:23-24 NIV

This is a foundational verse in Christianity. Believing in Jesus Christ, who was raised from the dead, justifies us before God. Our faith in Jesus allows us to be raised to life when Christ returns. Believe and you will be saved. But there is also an important secondary element which says that Christ must be our Lord. That means that we believe, *and* we follow or are subject to him. We obey what he asks us to do.

As a believer in Jesus, you also are asked to obey him. Even as you read his Word and pray today, you are walking in obedience to him. Make this practice a strong discipline in your life. It will be rewarded.

Jesus, I want to follow and obey you. Help me each day to put you first and to listen for your voice.

WHEN THE TIME COMES

I am convinced that nothing can ever separate us from God's love. Neither death nor life, neither angels nor demons, neither our fears for today nor our worries about tomorrow—not even the powers of hell can separate us from God's love.

ROMANS 8:38-39 NLT

Paul was an educated man. He was discipled as a Pharisee and raised in a Roman society. He was articulate and learned. He knew how to speak and how to debate for truth, which he demonstrated multiple times throughout his missionary journeys. Unlike most of us, he bled for his beliefs. He was truly a convicted man.

One day you may face persecution like Paul's, where speaking the truth costs you more than just public rebuke. You may have to bleed for it. It may cost you your life, as is happening around the world right now for many believers. This is the true cost of discipleship but be encouraged. You need not fear since God is preparing you for whatever you may face.

God, I want to be ready when the time comes so that I can answer my critics and stand up for the truth. Help me to be ready.

ACKNOWLEDGMENT

"I, Nebuchadnezzar, praise and exalt and glorify the King of heaven,
because everything he does is right and all his ways are just.
And those who walk in pride he is able to humble."
DANIEL 4:37 NIV

"Have you no dignity?" yelled the shopkeeper. The man was openly urinating in the street, unaware of the people streaming by. His coat was torn, and his matted hair was slightly covered by a tilted cap. He didn't care. Not long ago he was a different man; four years earlier to be exact. He was a top executive, controlling interests across the world and working in the upper floors of the very building he was now urinating on. As he drunkenly fumbled with his zipper, he recalled how he crashed so hard. It all started with a small act of deceit. One dishonorable act led to another. He turned, regretful of past choices.

Previously a distinguished man exalted by his peers, he was now a vagabond. Thinking about it more, he realized he lost his way when he was caught up in his own success. He no longer acknowledged the God who made him and gave him his honorable title. He was a modern-day Nebuchadnezzar.

God, help me to always acknowledge you. You are my God and I serve you first. My life belongs to you.

RETURNING

"The Spirit of truth. The world cannot accept him, because it neither sees him nor knows him. But you know him, for he lives with you and will be in you."
JOHN 14:17 NIV

The Bible makes it clear that deceit will be common in the final days of this world. Jesus encourages us not to be deceived but to be alert. He wants us to watch and to not be caught up in the hype of this age. The Holy Spirit is with us. He shows us what is deceitful and protects us from the devil. The more we live this life, the more we recognize the need for his truth, so we become sharpened and sensitive to his voice. This is how we will know when Jesus returns; his Spirit will confirm with our spirit. But we also should be careful not to be alone in this. We are to remain in the body of Christ so that we do not become deceived ourselves.

You are connected by God to other believers. It is good to know you have friends around you that believe the same and can encourage you in your faith. Continue to connect with them and talk about God's Word and the return of Jesus.

God, please fill me with your truth and help me to not be deceived. I want my heart and mind to be sharp when Jesus returns.

GUARDED HEART

"This people's heart has become calloused; they hardly hear with their ears, and they have closed their eyes. Otherwise they might see with their eyes, hear with their ears, understand with their hearts and turn, and I would heal them."

MATTHEW 13:15 NIV

Have you ever had one of those days when it seems that everything you say is taken the wrong way? Jesus did. He spoke clearly to those around him about his coming kingdom and his future reign. They still did not understand because for four hundred years Israel had been waiting for a savior. Jesus fit the bill, but he was not going to be their king immediately. He had future plans. They wanted to make him king right away. They had no ear to hear what he was saying, likely because they didn't want to believe it.

You must guard your heart from becoming hard. If you want something that God is not going to give you immediately, be willing to let it go. Trust in Jesus to deliver all of his promises in his own timing.

Jesus, give me patience and help me to guard my heart from disappointment in you. I want to trust you and wait for all good things to come in your timing.

FREE TO SERVE

You were called to freedom, brothers. Only do not use your freedom as an opportunity for the flesh, but through love serve one another. For the whole law is fulfilled in one word: "You shall love your neighbor as yourself."

GALATIANS 5:13-14 ESV

Freedom comes at a cost. For a country to be free, it is often established with the shed blood of its citizens. It cost lives for us to be free today. In Christ, it is no different. Apart from his shed blood we would not be free. A sad fact of humanity is that when liberty has passed through several generations, the cost is forgotten. And that same freedom is used to demand things that are self-serving.

Jesus knew this, and his disciples did too. They remind us here that our freedom came at a cost, and it should not be used to serve ourselves. As you go out into the world, find out how you can serve others. Use your freedom in Christ to love your neighbor, and most of all, love your family.

Jesus, thank you for the freedom I have in you. Thank you for the generations who came before me and paid for my freedom. Help me to use my freedom to serve others.

THE HEART IS FULL

If you declare with your mouth, "Jesus is Lord,"
and believe in your heart that God raised him from the dead,
you will be saved.

ROMANS 10:9 NIV

The Bible makes it clear that the heart is full of what the mouth speaks. When we talk and whatever we talk about is exactly what is on our minds and in our hearts. When we declare that Jesus is our Lord, we are saying that we are willingly subject to him. We follow him. We also believe in his death and resurrection. This is what it means to be a believer in Christ. We know that he is who he says he is, and we trust in him enough to do what he commands. We choose to do what Christ did, even to the point of death.

As you devote yourself to following Christ by loving him, his Word, his people, and his ways, you will end up dying to yourself. It is the natural process of sanctification. Be encouraged that Jesus knows and has been there. He will reward you for your choices.

Jesus, I want to follow you with all my heart. Help me to love you above myself. It is hard to let go, but you can help me to do so. I love you.

DESIRES MET

Jesus said to them, "I am the bread of life;
whoever comes to me shall not hunger,
and whoever believes in me shall never thirst."
JOHN 6:35 ESV

When you're an adolescent, there can be intense feelings of hunger at times. You become so ravenous you feel like you could eat a horse. Perhaps that saying came from an adolescent! When you are that hungry, look out pantry and fridge! It is amazing to watch how much you can consume before being satisfied. But when the eating is complete, the look of gratification, especially if you have been the cook, is satisfying in itself.

People who love cooking take delight in that look. Jesus, the best of all chefs, wants to fulfill the hunger in you. He delights in seeing you gratified too. When you come to him, he promises that you will never be hungry or thirsty again. That is a never-ending sense of contentment! Draw close to Jesus and allow him to fill you with the satisfaction that only he can provide.

Jesus, I want to draw close to you and have you meet my desires. Help me to look to you in times when I am tempted and when I am entertained with things that do not glorify you.

GRACE

In him we have redemption through his blood,
the forgiveness of sins, in accordance with the riches of God's grace.
EPHESIANS 1:7 ESV

God is gracious toward us even in our sinful state. How can he be so kind? It's because we have Jesus who redeemed us with his blood. It is clear in Scripture that none of us are without sin. It will plague us until we die. We can improve our state by seeking God with all our hearts and maturing in Christ. We will sin less, but we will still be separated from God by sinfulness. It is inescapable apart from the work of Christ on the cross.

None of us will ever be good enough to receive God's grace because of our own doing. We rely solely on Jesus Christ and his salvation. Your Savior is Jesus Christ. Focus on pleasing him, not avoiding sin. The more he is your focus, the less sin will hinder you.

Jesus, I want my heart and mind to be devoted to you, but I know that I am limited. Help me, Holy Spirit, to rely on your work in my life. I want to mature in Christ.

REPENT

God did this so that they would seek him and perhaps reach out
for him and find him, though he is not far from any one of us.
"For in him we live and move and have our being."

ACTS 17:27-28 NIV

Despite what some may say about God, he desires that all men are saved. Jesus came to save all people. He never turns anyone away who seeks him. There is not a predetermined qualifier that all people need to meet. It does not matter if you are a serial killer, a homeless man, or a child. All are welcome. That is the amazing thing about God. He accepts all and rejects none.

To come to Christ, you'll have to admit that you are a sinner in need of a Savior. That requires you to humble yourself, to turn from sin, and to obey Jesus. That's the part that a lot of people do not want to do. They want a God who accepts them and allows them to live their own way. You have surrendered your life to Jesus and can continue to grow in your obedience to him. This takes time. Maturity comes over the years, not overnight. Trust in him, pray, read the Word, and be with other believers.

Thank you, Jesus, for accepting me into your family. I want to do things your way. Help me to mature and to know you more.

NOT ANXIOUS

Be still in the presence of the LORD,
and wait patiently for him to act.
Don't worry about evil people
who prosper or fret about their wicked schemes.

PSALM 37:7 NLT

What does it mean to be still and wait? We would never get anything done. Yet time and time again, the Bible says to wait upon the Lord; to be still and patient. This stillness and waiting is not about being idle. As we know, the Bible also speaks clearly about the evils of being idle. So stillness is not about inactivity, but about tranquility. We can be at peace, knowing God will move on our behalf. We don't fret or allow ourselves to become anxious.

Maybe you want a new sports item, or a console, a computer, or even a car. Waiting may be about not purchasing that item right away, seeking the Lord for approval of the purchase, or praying for your attention and money to go elsewhere if it is not the Lord's will. Let God know that you are anxious to talk to him and allow him to be part of your decision-making process.

God, help me to be patient and not anxious about my future. I want, but I don't always need, and sometimes I require your help to determine what is important. Thank you for your help!

YOU SEE ALL

Cast your cares on the LORD and he will sustain you;
he will never let the righteous be shaken.

PSALM 55:22 NIV

We know godly men who encounter trouble, and they crumble to the ground in tears, anger, and hurt. But they don't stay there. They rise again. They find new resolve in seeking God, and they gain deeper maturity through the process. God never promises to remove all the hard things in life. In fact, he says that we will face them, but with difficulty will come his strength and his care. When we fall, he will pick us up. We will not be shaken.

You may be facing difficulty in your life at this time. Know that God never leaves you nor forsakes you because of your trouble. He is there to carry and care for you. Trust in him.

God, you do care about me. Help me to realize that even though I feel overwhelmed, you are not. You know what is happening in my life and you can take care of me. I trust in you.

WHOLESOME

A wholesome tongue is a tree of life,
But perverseness in it breaks the spirit.
PROVERBS 15:4 NKJV

Have you been around someone who makes you happy and when you walk away from conversations with them, you feel encouraged and uplifted? That person knows how to speak and encourage others. Their language is not dirty or discouraging. Contrast them with the person who swears consistently. They tear people down and talk negatively about life. It is hard to walk away from being with them and still have a positive outlook on life. Sometimes you get away from those conversations and feel somewhat liberated, almost like you escaped tyranny.

Your words matter. How you speak can give life to someone, or it can send them away with a broken spirit. Use words that encourage and speak kindness. Show others favor as God has favored you.

Father, help me to control my tongue. I know that without your Sprit working in me, I will make mistakes. Thank you for your forgiveness. Give me words of life for people and fill my mind with your thoughts.

SHELTERED

In the depths of my heart I truly know
that you, Yahweh, have become my Shield;
You take me and surround me with yourself.
Your glory covers me continually.
You lift high my head.

PSALM 3:3 TPT

It was early in the morning, and he awoke to the flash of lightning and the clap of thunder. He felt the house rumble and heard the rain splattering on the rooftop. The tin roof created a rhythmic sound that lulled him back to sleep. Snuggled up in his warm blanket, the boy slept the storm away awakening a second time to his mother's voice: "Breakfast, boys!"

In the middle of a great storm, it is such a comfort to be with family inside a warm house and a cozy bed, protected from the elements and insulated by love. This is the provision God has for us all. He covers, forgives sin, and welcomes us into his family. His love lifts our eyes to him, and we are sheltered.

God, thank you for keeping me and saving me from drowning in fear. I want to trust in you.

INTEGRITY

The eyes of the LORD are in every place,
Watching the evil and the good.
PROVERBS 15:3 NASB

The boy pleaded with his father to borrow his iPad. They were traveling, and he wanted to play while waiting for their flight to board. The father obliged, knowing that this trip would be dreary without something to do, and how could he not? He was, after all, playing on his phone. So, the two of them sat beside each other, but distant from each other on their devices. *Pling.* The husband's face flushed; a woman had propositioned him. Forgetting that his son had his other device, the man answered. The woman answered back. The man answered again, and it was over.

Years later, the son spoke to his dad in a moment of sobriety. "Dad, I remember when a woman asked you to…" The father remembered the moment with no shame at all. They talked about it for a while. What had the father said to the woman? Integrity is doing the right thing when no one is watching, or when you *think* no one is watching. You choose honor over shame. It is not easy; you fight your very nature to expose evil and choose righteousness, walking in integrity.

Help me to walk in integrity, God. I want to honor you in everything I do.

RUN WELL

I have fought the good fight,
I have finished the race,
I have kept the faith.

2 TIMOTHY 4:7 NCV

Paul was at the end of his life when he wrote this verse. He had suffered immensely throughout his life for the sake of the gospel. It wasn't because he fought with men physically, but because he was speaking the truth with power and authority. He was shipwrecked, bitten by a snake, beaten, and imprisoned. Through it all, he never doubted God or held him to task for his pain. He went through it because he loved God and served him. He kept his faith in Christ Jesus.

As you continue to seek God in a world where his truth is shunned and his Word is marginalized, be encouraged that God is with you. Love him even if you have to suffer because you know that what he has for you is much better than what this world can offer. Run the good race and finish for the prize of resurrection.

Jesus, I want to be like Paul and say at the end of my life that I have kept my faith and run well. Help me to trust in you in the most difficult times, not just when things are good.

FREED TO FOLLOW

God has made all things new, and reconciled us to himself,
and given us the ministry of reconciling others to God.

2 CORINTHIANS 5:18 TPT

He was a man devoted to serving others. While living with his wife and children, their home was filled with strangers needing help. He was a businessman who traveled the countryside but also spent time sharing Christ. After years of seeing so many of the same people returning to seek salvation and watching them struggle, he decided something needed to be done. Searching far and wide, he found a large farm on an island where he could start discipling those trapped in lifestyles of addiction. He swapped his home, business, and some cash, for a piece of property. Then he moved his family there and began slowly bringing men and women to their new community.

It was hard work and sacrificial living, but it became a place of promise for those lost to the streets. The man asked for nothing in return for his work except to see that people loved God passionately and were freed from the habits that had stopped them from following Christ forever.

Jesus, help me to share your love with others and to let them know about you.

FOR THE PROMISES

He has granted to us his precious and very great promises, so that through them you may become partakers of the divine nature, having escaped from the corruption that is in the world because of sinful desire.

2 PETER 1:4 ESV

It was a perilous adventure. He had traveled across rugged mountains where paths fell away at each step, escaped carnivorous animals who ravenously tracked him, and traversed raging waters that attempted to drown him. Along the way, many had tried to entice him to stay. "Take it easy, just rest here." It seemed at every turn he faced adversity, yet he was determined not to be dissuaded. His promise of a kingdom that was so vast and great was what kept him pressing onward. Though he was exhausted, his dreams of what lay ahead kept him steady.

You face a world that tries to entice you constantly. You will face battles throughout your life that will make you want to quit. Hold fast to the promises of God. Like the man in this story, you have an incredible kingdom to inherit.

God, help me to be strong in the face of struggle. I want to have an easy, successful road, but I know that is not the life of a Jesus- follower. Help me persevere in order to receive your promises!

EMPOWERING GRACE

God continues to give us more grace. That's why Scripture says,
"God opposes those who are proud.
But he gives grace to those who are humble."
JAMES 4:6 ESV

God is gracious. Your own father figure may not be. Somehow, we twist these two together like a fishing line after a bad cast. It takes time to unravel our father figure from God. But God is gracious. He is kind. He loves unconditionally because he is love. His grace empowers us in our weaknesses, for that is what grace does: it allows weakness to exist so we can be strengthened by it.

Because of your father, or because of your own fears, you may not allow weakness to show in yourself. This can result in you becoming internally ungracious and mean to those around you. Through humility of heart and recognition of brokenness, you can embrace grace. Grace gives you the strength you need to change. You can become one who demonstrates from the inside out, the goodness of graciousness.

God, I want to be gracious like you, but I struggle. Help me to recognize how much grace I am given so that I can give it freely.

MIGHTY

That power is the same as the mighty strength he exerted when he raised Christ from the dead and seated him at his right hand in the heavenly realms, far above all rule and authority, power and dominion, and every name that is invoked, not only in the present age but also in the one to come.

EPHESIANS 19:21 NIV

Not to be confused with authoritarian, *authoritative* is positive in its meaning. It means to be able to be trusted, to be confident and commanding in a good way. This is the person who knows what they are talking about and is reliable in what they say. It is like the captain who sailed for years talking to a new ship hand. It's the reason the rookie quarterback will listen to the GOAT talk about football. It is a man who owns multiple companies sharing with new businessmen. The finest example of being authoritative is seen in Jesus Christ. He is the ultimate authority. He knows all things and is able to do all things.

Just as God is the authority on all good things, he wants you to be confident of his power and ability within you. Know that God is with you today and his mighty strength is supporting you.

Father, thank you for helping me in this life. I know you are strengthening me even when I don't recognize it. Thank you for your goodness.

ATTENTIVE

Love each other with genuine affection
and take delight in honoring each other.
ROMANS 12:10 NLT

When Scripture says to give honor to one another, what does it look like practically? It simply means that we demonstrate regard for others' needs before we consider our own. It's not just practical, but it's also spiritual and emotional. This can be where it cuts us the most, and where we actually struggle to honor one another. It is not common for us to pay attention to our emotions, but we need this practice in order to mature in all three areas. When we do pay attention, what we may notice is that we say and do things that do not honor others. We protect ourselves by putting other people down.

As you mature, you will become more attentive to your emotional state, and you can better love those around you. You will be a stable influence in their lives, having regard for them emotionally. This is what it means to truly give honor to one another.

Jesus, as I mature, help me to honor others and to love them as well as you did. Holy Spirit, fill me afresh so that I can walk as Jesus did on this earth.

NEVER GIVE UP

We are surrounded by a great cloud of people whose lives tell us what faith
means. So let us run the race that is before us and never give up.
HEBREWS 12:1 NCV

When you think of a great man, who do you think of? Perhaps you
consider a sportsperson or a singer, A scientist or a philanthropist?
What about great spiritual people? Perhaps a grandparent comes to
mind, or someone else in your family. Maybe your pastor has captured
your respect? There are many around us who can inspire us to do better.
Often we see them and wonder how we could be like them. We admire
those attributes that we like in them and think about the ways we could
do what they do. We all want to be great at something. We all want
recognition.

You can be great. Those who are hardworking, determined, diligent, and
patient are often the ones who become great at something. Few are the
famous and lucky without those other characteristics. Work hard at your
faith and persevere. You will be rewarded greatly by God.

*I want to be famous for something, God. I want to do something great.
Most of all I want to please you. Help me to work hard at doing that first.*

KINDNESS

Be kind to one another, tenderhearted,
forgiving one another, as God in Christ forgave you.
EPHESIANS 4:32 ESV

The lad wanted a dog so badly. He had played at friends' houses and seen how much fun they were. They went with you everywhere and they were always happy to greet you. He wanted a buddy like that. He went out on his bike to cruise a bit. He enjoyed listening to the sound of the wind whistling by. Faster, faster he rode. He wanted the wind to roar like a jet. That would mean he was going really fast. Suddenly he heard a different sound—a whimper, or a cry maybe? He slowed down quickly, listening for the sound again. There, over in the bush, he saw a brown patch. He cautiously approached and found a young dog, small and bloodied, with its leg twisted. He bent down and patted its head, tears rolling down his cheeks.

The next summer, the boy was out on his bike again. This time he didn't care about the wind; he laughed with deep joy as his buddy ran beside him. Kindness shows up in humanity in many ways. It is simple compassion and consideration for those we encounter in life. You can be kind by helping others and improving their circumstances through thoughtful acts.

Thank you for your kindness to me, God. Help me to be aware of those around me who are in need so that I can help them.

IDENTITY

He saved us, not because of works done by us in righteousness, but according to his own mercy, by the washing of regeneration and renewal of the Holy Spirit.
TITUS 3:5 ESV

As we grow up, who we identify with changes. We start out life by mimicking our parents in words, actions, and persona. By the time we are about five years old, our personalities are set. It is just a matter of being developed and guided after that. As we enter our middle childhood years, we start comparing ourselves with friends and want to be like them. Our identity forms by our social connections. This especially occurs in the adolescent years where rejection of the parental modeling naturally occurs. Within certain boundaries, it is a healthy aspect of this age. We are raised to leave home and find our way in the world. A parent's job is to guide children, to love them into their own identity, and to see them become healthy individuals.

Through the years that you have lived so far, God has been with you. He has guided you, cried with you, laughed with you, and watched you go through all your joys and struggles. He identifies the characteristics that he has planted in you as gifts given to accomplish the tasks that he has prepared for you. Your distinctive, unique personality combined with your gifts are not a mistake.

Thank you for how you have made me, God. I ask that my life would serve you well.

WARFARE

We give thanks to God always for all of you,
constantly mentioning you in our prayers.
1 THESSALONIANS 1:2 ESV

We don't see when angels and demons are battling against each other. It would be a sight for sure. We may sometimes encounter spiritual events that we confuse with some unnatural phenomenon. But we can be sure that both spiritual powers are at work consistently. One marches to God's orders and the other follows Satan's command. Somewhere in the middle of this roaring battle sits the earth and humanity, mostly unaware.

The apostle Paul was aware of this battle and was constantly in prayer for himself and those he served. We also need to be alert to the spiritual realm. It is in the place of prayer where we understand the powers at work, and we comprehend the greatness of our God. You are a spiritual being. You have within you the power of Christ who overcame all the enemy's power. As you go about your day, pray for God to open your eyes to all he is doing.

God, help me to see beyond the flesh. Give me eyes to see what you are doing spiritually and awaken my heart to prayer.

BRAVERY OVER TIME

"Here's what I've learned through it all:
Don't give up; don't be impatient;
be entwined as one with the Lord.
Be brave and courageous, and never lose hope.
Yes, keep on waiting—for he will never disappoint you!"
PSALM 27:14 TPT

Growing up on a remote island had its charms and its difficulties. But to this young boy, it was full of adventure and delight. A few challenges still remained. His first was overcoming his older brother who taunted him with devious plans of misadventure. There were late night walks with animal skulls hidden in the bushes, spooky moments in shady woods, and chases across farmland by animals and other foes. Nothing was more challenging than going out into the ocean where sharks slashed, eels eerily lurked, and stingrays swarmed the surf.

His bravery was learned, not in one moment, but over time. His father, in whom he put his complete trust, patiently led him step- by- step to surf, snorkel, fish, sail, and eventually enjoy the ocean. His memory of these experiences enabled him to realize the depth of fear he had overcome. He had overcome fear through trust, patience, and firm action.

Father, help me to trust you, to know that you are with me. Show me how I can be brave.

DYNAMITE

"You will receive power when the Holy Spirit comes on you;
and you will be my witnesses in Jerusalem, and in all Judea and Samaria,
and to the ends of the earth."

ACTS 1:8 NIV

Jesus, speaking to his disciples, explained what was going to happen to them in the near future. They had no idea about the power of the Holy Spirit to transform lives and to dynamically impact each of them personally. The Holy Spirit is active today working in the hearts of every believer, and as the day of Christ's return draws near he will be increasing his activity. Christ is looking for those who are devoted to him in order to use them mightily to do miracles and to display the glory of God.

Prepare your heart to be dynamically changed as the Holy Spirit comes upon you. Ask for him to baptize you freshly and to fill you with his awesome power. Devote yourself to the pursuit of God, so you are one of those he calls upon before the return of Christ. He wants you!

Holy Spirit, fill me and change me. Help me to be devoted to Jesus and to pursue him with all my heart. Make me ready for his return.

BRILLIANCE

The Lord God is brighter than the brilliance of a sunrise!
Wrapping himself around me like a shield,
he is so generous with his gifts of grace and glory.
Those who walk along his paths with integrity
will never lack one thing they need, for he provides it all!
PSALM 84:11 TPT

It was a chilly winter morning. His head was tucked away from the biting wind. When he turned his head to look for the sun, the breeze stole his breath away. He sat in a stand waiting for his prey to walk unknowingly before him, but before it did, he desperately needed the sun to rise. There it was. He felt its warmth as it brilliantly shimmered across the ice to his left. As the sun climbed, his body was embraced by the radiant heat, and he almost forgot why he was there. Between the warmth of the sun and the majesty of God's creation, his prey was forgotten. He glorified God for the beauty of the morning.

You are a part of God's brilliant creation. You were no mistake, and he takes delight in you. As you look to him, he will always provide what you need.

Father, I believe in you. I love what you have made. I am made by you, and I ask that you would continue to provide all that I need today.

NOT A LIAR

*Or do you despise the riches of His goodness, forbearance, and longsuffering,
not knowing that the goodness of God leads you to repentance?*
ROMANS 2:4 NKJV

God is not a man that he should lie. He is not a man that he should
fail. He doesn't break his promises. He is good. He is love. He is just.
Fellowship with him means that we remain in the presence of a patient
and kind Father who tolerates our many sins. Why? Because of the
sacrifice and the righteous offering of his Son, Jesus Christ.

The riches of his goodness are found in this offering, and because of this
sacrifice God is patient with us. He suffers willingly to wait for the end of
all things. He is not pleased about our continued sin, but in his kindness,
he allows time for our repentance. None of us are without sin. We fail
every day in the standard he sets for us. When we recognize his mercy,
we can turn to him to find grace and forgiveness. It is God's goodness
that leads you to repentance. He is for you. He has established you on a
path that leads you closer to him.

*Father, thank you for your goodness and kindness. I repent of my ways and
ask you to lead me. I surrender my heart to you again today.*

SYMBOLS

The LORD said to him, "Who has made man's mouth? Or who makes him mute or deaf, or seeing or blind? Is it not I, the LORD? Now then go, and I, even I, will be with your mouth, and teach you what you are to say."

EXODUS 4:11-12 NIV

When we let fear control us, we forget that God made us. It's as if he may not know what we are going through, or that he wouldn't understand our difficulties. Other times we just don't think about him at all. We are afraid. That is when we get ourselves into the most trouble. Somehow, we need to remember our Creator and have his presence always before us. When we do, and we recall how great and marvelous he is, we can be confident.

This is why Israel had instructions to have symbols and ornaments on their hands and foreheads. They would be working with their hands or talking with a neighbor and be reminded of him. Symbols and habits give us the ability to keep the Lord always before us. Our faith is full of healthy symbols and traditions for this reason.

Father, thank you for good habits that have been formed in my faith. I pray that no symbol or tradition would become an idol, but that they would help to keep you always before me.

CHOOSING FRIENDS

Speaking the truth in love, we will grow to become in every respect the mature body of him who is the head, that is, Christ. From him the whole body, joined and held together by every supporting ligament, grows and builds itself up in love, as each part does its work.

EPHESIANS 4:15-16 NIV

It has been said that you cannot become spiritually mature and remain emotionally immature. For men this is a difficult saying because we struggle to acknowledge our feelings as much as we should, and we do not share with each other as much as women do. Typically, women use a lot more words and expressions. When it comes to growing emotionally, what do we need so we can also grow spiritually? The picture Paul gives here is helpful in explaining that it is the whole body of Christ that matures, and each part contributes. Our maturing is not done alone; it is part of a whole process in a body.

If you are to mature emotionally, you need connection with others to stimulate and sharpen your emotional awareness. Seek out healthy friendships and godly people to walk out life with.

Jesus, I ask that you would help me to be with other believers. Please help me choose my friends wisely.

BOW THE KNEE

At the name of Jesus every knee should bow, of those in heaven, and of those on earth, and of those under the earth, and that every tongue should confess that Jesus Christ is Lord, to the glory of God the Father.

PHILIPPIANS 2:10-11 NKJV

There is not a soul on earth who has been, is, or ever will be, who will avoid bowing the knee to Christ. Every person will be resurrected to life and will face the judgment seat of God. All humanity will bow before Jesus. We cannot escape this reality. So, why doesn't every person surrender to him today? He is good, loving, just, kind, and merciful. He wants to improve lives, not destroy them. Why wouldn't we all surrender to someone who loves us and gives of themselves to benefit our lives? It is because we are all, at our core, rebellious. We want control, we want pleasure, we don't want someone telling us what to do or what not to do.

You have chosen the better thing. Following Christ makes you a better person at loving others and pleasing God. Plus, there are great rewards waiting for you when you are resurrected into eternal life!

Jesus, I surrender to you. I believe in you, your death, your resurrection, and your authority. Help me to continue to follow you and to love others well.

EVERLASTING

Long ago you laid the foundation of the earth and made the heavens with your hands. They will perish, but you remain forever; they will wear out like old clothing. You will change them like a garment and discard them. But you are always the same; you will live forever.

PSALM 102:25-27 NIV

God is eternal. When we ponder that it blows our minds. How long has he been around? He has existed for eternity. Imagine what that looks like. What has he been doing all that time? It hurts the mind to think on it too long. But what we can know, and not need to guess at, is his character.

God is creative, merciful, powerful, patient, kind, just, and unconditionally loving. There is no measure on his ability to exercise his character. He doesn't tire, and he doesn't get emotionally frazzled. Your parents, siblings, and friends do. They all have limits. But God never does. He remains constant always. You are connected to the constant one, the everlasting God. He holds you in his hands and gives you strength each day. Trust in him. Trust in his unchanging character.

God, I want to know you more and I need your help to trust you. Help me to know your strength each day, and especially today.

WARRIOR

Put on every piece of God's armor so you will be able to resist the enemy in the time of evil. Then after the battle you will still be standing firm.

EPHESIANS 6:13 NLT

When you think of those who are valiant, who comes to your mind? Likely you'll think of the brave war hero or the fictional character who beat back a villain. You may be able to picture scenes in your mind and feel the strength they demonstrated as they pushed forth and overcame their adversary. How many of us think of the person in their room praying and interceding for others? At first thought it may not seem very bold. But if we truly grasped the spiritual world around us, and if we understood the battles occurring in the heavens right now, we would appreciate that there is courage in intercession; there is bravery in prayer.

You have within you the power of a prayer warrior. Be encouraged by the Holy Spirit to speak with authority in prayer. Find believers who know how to pray this way and, like a warrior in training, learn from them.

God, help me find believers who know how to pray powerfully. I want to pray and see your will be done. I want to see strongholds pulled down in Jesus' name.

SEASONED

Show yourself in all respects to be a model of good works, and in your teaching show integrity, dignity, and sound speech that cannot be condemned, so that an opponent may be put to shame, having nothing evil to say about us.
TITUS 2:7-8 ESV

There are men in our lives that command respect. Some of them are young, successful individuals, and others are seasoned with salt-and-pepper hair. The best are the elders; fully greyed or bald. They are calm, respectful, patient, and they demonstrate consideration of others. Even when they have strong opinions on matters, they wait to express them. If they don't have the opportunity to speak, they would rather listen anyway. It provokes greater thought within themselves.

These men ponder the life of the young man they used to be and how much they have learned since that time. Their actions are intentionally self-sacrificing, strengthening others even at their own expense. The objective of their lives is to finish well, serving others so they have the confidence and muster to pass the same characteristics on to the next generation.

Jesus, help me to respect my elders and to give them honor. I want to learn and not turn away from them. Remind me of how much I need to listen to their wisdom.

POWER IN YOUR WALK

"Stand firm, and you will win life."
LUKE 21:19 NIV

Jesus is our life. He promises that if we stand firm, he will be there
to back us up. Right now, he looks out over the earth for those who
seek him, and he promises to strongly support those whose hearts are
completely his. He is a man of his Word. He is God, and he does not lie.
We are able to stand firm because of his example to us, and because we
have the same Spirit in us; the Holy Spirit who strengthened him and
gave him power lives in us today. We can win at life because we are given
the same Spirit that Jesus had to live.

You have the Spirit of Christ in you. There is nothing that separates you
from him except your own choice to deny him. But you do not; you have
chosen to embrace Christ and follow him. Today as you walk out the
door, remember who is within you and win at life!

*Jesus, thank you for your Spirit within me. Help me today to walk in your
authority and power. Give me your words to speak and teach me how to
love and serve as you do.*

SEE AND DO

Do not neglect to do good and to share what you have,
for such sacrifices are pleasing to God.
HEBREWS 13:16 ESV

What is it about helping people that brings us satisfaction? There is a natural release of different body chemicals God created in each of us called dopamine, serotonin, and oxytocin. They are feel-good hormones and they do feel good. When we hear a baby crying, someone scream, a siren go off, or the yelp of an animal, we are alerted to trouble. It grasps our attention, and we jump into action. This is because of adrenaline, another hormone that God made which helps us to act. We were made to be helpful and kind and to act on the natural responses of our bodies.

You have inside of you these hormones that help you to act and to feel good about it. It can be the simple act of holding open a door, helping with groceries, or taking care of a sibling. Look for people who have needs and assist them. Then feel the goodness that God made flow through you. Enjoy your act of service.

God, thank you for how you made me. I know that I can do more for others if I can stop thinking about myself first. Help me to see the needs of others and act on them.

PERCEIVING DANGER

The Lord is my light and my salvation—
so why should I be afraid?
The Lord is my fortress,
protecting me from danger,
so why should I tremble?
PSALM 27:1 NLT

Have you ever seen a mother who was watching someone or some situation, suddenly grab their child and walk away? They may have saved their child from harm. Or perhaps a female in your family tells you when there is danger nearby; she senses trouble. These are survival instincts that initiate the response system to be more wary and protective. They are good when they are balanced with confidence in God. But when driven by fear, this sensitivity and discernment can become paralyzing.

Our lives are like this with so many of our traits and gifts. God looks for you to operate in the strengths that he has placed within you, but you are also responsible to make sure that they are balanced by the Holy Spirit. He gives peace, joy, love, and kindness to you so when you do perceive something potentially harmful, you can be calm and listen to him. He will guide you in how best to respond.

Holy Spirit, I am glad that you are a part of my life. Help me to listen to you and to follow your leading.

BEHAVING WITH HONOR

She is clothed with strength and dignity,
and she laughs without fear of the future.
When she speaks, her words are wise,
and she gives instructions with kindness.
PROVERBS 31:25-26 NLT

We are forever connected to our mothers. Our first oxygen came through them, our blood was shared with them, and the first things we heard were their heartbeats and voices. Mothers are incredibly valuable. Every human, whether they believe in him or not, receives their life from God. Our breath, our blood, all of our lives belong to him. He started it and he will be there when it finishes. We are forever connected to him.

Despite your current feelings for your mom, which can change from day to day, God asks you to honor her. As you go about your day today, find ways to honor your mother. Honor is given mostly by obeying what she asks you to do, such as cleaning up after yourself. But you can also show her favor by going the extra mile. Do more than just what is asked and bless her today.

Father, help me to love my mother like you do. When I am angry at her or upset with her decisions, help me to keep honoring her.

EXPECTATIONS

Hope deferred makes the heart sick,
but a dream fulfilled is a tree of life.
PROVERBS 13:12 NIV

It is said that the greater the expectations, the greater the disappointment. Hope in this life is fickle. So, do we all do away with our expectations so that we are never disappointed? No, having expectations is part of being human. Life would be awful without hope. Problems occur when our hope and our expectations are placed in things that are not trustworthy. If we can learn to place less importance on the things happening in this life and more importance on the promises that God has made to us, we will find greater satisfaction in life.

God wants you to expect him to show up. He likes meeting expectations. He promises that when we seek him, we will find him. If you set your heart on him, then your desires will also become his desires, and they will be met.

God, I want to get so close to you that I know your heart and your desires for my life. If we can get there together, I will never be disappointed. When I am sad, please lift me up and remind me of your faithfulness.

NEW

If anyone is in Christ, he is a new creation.
The old has passed away; behold, the new has come.
1 CORINTHIANS 5:17 ESV

When we say that a person is in Christ, it means that person has acknowledged Jesus as Lord, as God, and believes in his death and resurrection. They believe that he died for their sins, and they are full of gratitude and praise. They know they are a new creation because things are different within them, not just how they behave, but also their very deepest thoughts and desires. We can all experience newness like this in our lives. Christ works in us to renew us to be more like him on an ongoing basis. He is the creator of new.

As you draw close to God today, and as you humble your heart before him, ask for a new revelation of what he is doing in you. Confidently know that he is working in you to make you a better follower of his.

Jesus, I choose to follow you and I ask that you would reveal new things that you are doing in my life. Sometimes my life is crowded with other things. Help me to be less distracted. I want to focus on you.

DECENT

"Love your enemies, and do good, and lend, expecting nothing in return,
and your reward will be great, and you will be sons of the Most High,
for he is kind to the ungrateful and the evil."

LUKE 6:35 ESV

Decent. It may not be the most complimentary word. How did he play? He was decent. No one wants to play sports decently. We want to play them well. A decent sports player is just okay, right? He's not the best. You would pick them midway through selection. How was the restaurant? It was decent. What a great movie! Nah, I thought it was decent.

When it comes to social context though, we hope that we present ourselves decently. We want our family to be decent, especially if we invite a sibling over to a girlfriend's place. Or even more so our parents. *Please be decent. Don't make corny jokes and share stories about me.* Be civilized and well mannered. Be respectful and polite. These are the basic principles of human decency. As a believer, you want to demonstrate decency in all situations. It affects how others see God. Decency and honor for others goes a long way in sharing the love of God.

Father, help me to represent you well to others. I am a follower of Christ and I want that to be shown to others in how I behave.

DEMONSTRATE LOVE

"You shall love the LORD your God with all your heart and with all your soul
and with all your mind and with all your strength."

MARK 12:30 ESV

Jesus is worthy of all our love. But what measures love? It is a combination of many things: focus, attention, devotion, faithfulness, endurance, and loyalty. Love is demonstrated by all of these, which is why when God commands us to love him first, he asks for us to do so with all of our hearts, souls, minds, and strength. Disciples who love Jesus make him a priority in their lives, and they rid themselves of all other distractions. Second to this commandment was to love others similarly. It is a natural outcome in our lives that when we love God this well, we pour out love to others in a similar fashion.

If you want to truly love others well, focus your affection on God. Get rid of other distractions that take away from your devotion to him. Be the disciple that makes a difference for Christ.

Jesus, I want to love you so well that it is evident in my life. I want your love to overflow from me toward others so that they can know you also.

NECESSARY CAUTION

Be very careful how you live.
Do not live like those who are not wise,
but live wisely.
EPHESIANS 5:15 NCV

Being careful can be borne out of fear or indecision, but it can also be about watchful and necessary caution. As believers in Christ, our caution should be against becoming lazy in our faith and distracted by entertainment. If we are not alert, we can easily fall prey to a form of Christianity that has no power. Our power comes in the form of the Holy Spirit who is also our source of wisdom. This is why Paul calls us to live wisely; he encourages us to have lives that are filled with the Holy Spirit. To live this way, we are to be disciplined and alert, focused on what Jesus is doing. Additionally, we are to be ready for Jesus to return.

At times, your life can be distracting. God understands this and loves you despite your failings. He can handle you struggling, but he wants you to remember to continue inviting him into your life during your struggles. Allow him to be present and to speak to you.

Father, thank you for helping me to live in obedience to your Word. Help me to trust you and to hear you.

MONEY

"Well, then," Jesus said, "give to Caesar what belongs to Caesar, and give to God what belongs to God." His reply completely amazed them.

MARK 12:17 NLT

As you get older and start making money, you will find all sorts of ways to spend it. It is surprising how quickly it goes and what it is spent on. But when you start working, your employers will ask you about taxes. How much is going to be taken out of your paycheck? It is often shocking to see that chunk of your hard work that goes into the pocket of the government. It is their right to collect on services rendered to the citizens of any country. All of the public services we take for granted are paid for and managed by different government entities.

Jesus was challenged a few times regarding this. Why should the Israelites give money to the Romans? He gave such a simple answer. Render to Caesar what is due him. The Romans made the roads and provided services. Why did he say this so confidently? Because he knew that all he needed came from God. The government can have their bit, but we trust in our heavenly Father for all that we need God wants you to trust in him. Trust God. He will take care of you.

Father, I ask that you would help me to look to you in all my financial decisions. I want to believe that you will take care of me no matter what my situation is.

DESPITE THE KNOCKS

Recognize the value of every person and continually show love to every believer.
Live your lives with great reverence and in holy awe of God. Honor your rulers.

1 PETER 2:17 TPT

You are a great at sports, or maybe you're not? You're great at school, or maybe you're not? What is your worth, or where do you find it? Some psychologists say that the concept of self-esteem is negatively valuing. That means that you rate yourself based on a scale that seems to move; it depends on how you are accomplishing tasks or how you relate to others. Even worse it often leads to comparisons. When things are going well, subjectively, you have higher esteem. Yet, it only takes a few knocks and bumps, and your esteem can go down. What is your worth when relationships are bad, and you are not feeling accomplished?

You are esteemed by God. He loves you, his creation, and you are valued by him. No man or woman should ever be in a place of utter despair because of God's great love. Life can knock you down, but with a good community of believers around you, you can be encouraged and begin to understand your worth.

Jesus, please continue to speak your words of truth into my life. Help me to be surrounded by those who speak for you. Keep those who speak deception away from me.

LOVED BY THE KING

While we were still weak, at the right time Christ died for the ungodly. For one will scarcely die for a righteous person—though perhaps for a good person one would dare even to die—but God shows his love for us in that while we were still sinners, Christ died for us.

ROMANS 5:6-8 NIV

What a great love we share! God, our Creator, gave up his heavenly dwelling and became a dependent baby with no power. He became subject to his mother and father, obeying them and following them. Jesus, God of the universe, obeyed his *human* parents, whom he made! Wait, read that again. Why would the King of the universe subject himself like this? If we were in his shoes, would we give up our power or our position? But he did because of love. He not only humbled himself like this, but he also suffered immensely by bleeding and dying on a cross. He suffered mental, emotional, and physical trauma to such an extent that it eventually killed him. That is love.

You are loved by the King of the universe. He humbled himself and suffered so that you could know his love. Remind yourself of that today.

Jesus, thank you for all that you did on my behalf. I am loved by you, and I pray that you would help me to remember that throughout today.

JOB TO LEARN

The fear of the LORD is the beginning of knowledge,
but fools despise wisdom and instruction.
PROVERBS 1:7 NIV

As adolescents it is our job to learn. It should be a lifelong pursuit, but our brains are particularly hungry for learning in our teens. We also have a strong urge to become independent. When these two things combine, we can become overconfident in our new knowledge and less teachable. In our minds, we have it all together.

It is important, especially as believers, to keep ourselves humble. We need to listen to our elders and receive wisdom from them graciously. The fear of the Lord is found in admitting that we are learning, and that he knows it all; we do not. That is what starts us down a path of wisdom. Bring yourself before God today and admit that you don't know all that you need to know. Ask him to teach you and guide you into a life of wisdom.

God, I don't know everything. I don't really know much about life because I am so young. Teach me your wisdom and help me to respect those who have lived so much longer than I have.

PREPARED

Be alert and of sober mind. Your enemy the devil prowls around
like a roaring lion looking for someone to devour.

1 PETER 5:8 NIV

The parents relaxed on the couch, knowing their son was asleep. They
mistakenly assumed he had stayed in his toddler bed, but he slept
peacefully at the top of the stairs just out of sight. While they talked, a
disruptive thumping sound grew louder and closer. Having rolled over
in his sleep, their son was now flopping down each step like a rag doll.
Decisively and without hesitation, the father leapt over the couch, slid
across the wood floor, and caught the boy before he hit the hard landing,
his head mere inches away from the corner post.

Being alert is important on many levels. It is critical to watch and listen,
so we are ready to respond. We need to be ready and not taken by
surprise with circumstances or possibilities. You have internal response
systems that are made for bursts of powerful energy, and a large part of
your role is to be protective. God has put within you the strength needed
for every task.

*Father, thank you for helping me to be ready. I want to stay alert to my
environment and especially with what you are doing around the world.
Help me to be prepared for your return.*

BRINGING PURPOSE TO LIGHT

Their purpose is to teach people to live disciplined and successful lives,
to help them do what is right, just, and fair.

PROVERBS 1:3 NLT

It makes sense that we want to be known. We do not want to be truly
alone where no one understands us or loves us for who we are. But once
that is secured, we long for something to do. We have never been able
to sit idle. Even those who have nothing to do end up doing something.
The sad truth is that people with nothing to do end up making poor
decisions.

So, we have these two deep needs in being known and having a purpose.
God knows us, but do we know our purpose? That is a lifelong quest
because it often changes during different seasons of our lives. Reflect on
your brief life so far. Did your drive to do something shift? Perhaps you
changed activities or career ideas? Sometimes it is hard to know exactly
what your purpose is. At your core, your purpose is to seek God. When
you do, he reveals what he wants you to do. In this place of seeking, you
will find that you are known by the one who made you, and you will
accomplish what you are designed to do.

*God, help me to seek you first and trust that you will bring my purpose to
light.*

STAND IN DIFFICULTY

When Moses' hands grew tired, they took a stone and put it under him and he
sat on it. Aaron and Hur held his hands up—one on one side, one on the other—
so that his hands remained steady till sunset.

EXODUS 17:12 NIV

God knows that we need friends. None of us are to be alone because
we were made for relationships. It is especially important for us to have
a group that we belong to. The story about Moses in the verse above
demonstrates the importance of relationships. On his own, Moses would
have fainted from weariness. But the men around Moses helped him
to stay strong even to the point of holding up his arms. They were his
strength. We need friends who are able to stand with us in difficulty and
help us go through the worst of times, sometimes even holding us up.

Your faith family is the best place for you to be encouraged and uplifted
in your walk with God. They will strengthen you when you are having
difficulty, and they will empower you to keep going when you are weak.

*Father, thank you for my friends who know and love you. Help me to be an
encouragement to my friends.*

RECOGNIZED

Christ suffered for our sins once for all time. He never sinned, but he died for sinners to bring you safely home to God. He suffered physical death, but he was raised to life in the Spirit.

1 PETER 3:18 NLT

Certain days in the year are set aside to remember those who gave their lives fighting for freedom. We designate a day for these brave people to acknowledge their sacrifice. Some were conscripted into service not of their own accord, but they ended up dying bravely. Others went willingly to fight for freedom. Still others signed up to be with their buddies or brothers. They traversed lands that were not their own, and they suffered with cold, anxiety, hunger, and pain. They were most often spurred on in order to avoid the clutches of death. These brave men and women found no escape. They died in a land that was not their own, away from family and friends and after much suffering.

Our Savior knows what they experienced. He, too, suffered like them, away from his Father and in a place that was foreign to him. He knew us, but he was not like us in our sin. He died to save the world.

Father, thank you for those who suffered and sacrificed for my freedom, and most especially for Jesus Christ.

LIVING ON BREAD

"People do not live by bread alone,
but by every word that comes from the mouth of God."
MATTHEW 4:4 NLT

This may seem like an odd statement. How do you get life from words? Do they somehow fill you up? The reality is that everything we know exists because of God's word. We were made at his command. Everything is tied to what he spoke and continues to speak. At his word, the whole of heaven and earth was created and could be destroyed.

God's Word is true, and he is not a liar. Every promise that he has made will come true. One of those promises is that he will feed and clothe us, which is why we are not to live chasing after things that he will take care of. We can live on his Word, following his voice, and finding out how faithful he is to take care of us. The Lord promises to keep you and take care of you. You do not have to worry about tomorrow. Obey him today and listen for his voice. He is with you.

God, help me to hear your voice and to be attentive to your word. Help me to read my Bible, understand your ways, and remember your promises.

INFINITE

How great is our God!
There's absolutely nothing his power cannot accomplish,
and he has an infinite understanding of everything.
PSALM 147:5 ESV

God has an infinite understanding of everything. Nothing is beyond his comprehension, and he made all that existed. It may blow our minds, but he knows it all. He is great and there is no one who compares to him. If we find security in relationships with people, perhaps with friends or even with parents, it brings a sense of security because they have demonstrated consistent care and have earned our trust. God is trustworthy. He never fails; he never leaves us. He is faithful in all aspects.

You can know the goodness and greatness of God as you take time to read Scripture and spend time with others talking about him. Discover who he is, understand his character, and ask the Holy Spirit to reveal God the Father to you.

Holy Spirt, thank you for helping me to learn the truth. Show me more of the Father. Help me to understand Scripture and hunger for it more.

QUALIFIED

It is not that we think we are qualified to do anything on our own.
Our qualification comes from God.

2 CORINTHIANS 3:5 NLT

Have you ever had an interview? Some of the questions may be like the following: Why are you interested in this job? What experience do you have? Why do you think you are qualified ? If you have ever been interviewed you, have probably been asked about your qualifications. What does the hiring company really want to hear? They want to know if you can competently and skillfully complete the tasks related to the roles and responsibilities of the job.

Paul writes to the church at Corinth that his qualifications do not come from himself but from God. It's kind of a moot point because it is evident in the power and anointing of the Holy Spirit in his life. You are qualified to minister not because of who you are but because God is doing the work through you. You can prevent God's work by not walking according to his Spirit. Listen to the Holy Spirit and trust in him to work through you.

Father, help me to listen to the Holy Spirit and obey him. I want to trust in what you ask me to do.

HOSPITABLE HEART

"I was hungry and you gave me food,
I was thirsty and you gave me something to drink,
I was a stranger and you welcomed me."
MATTHEW 25:35 NRSV

In some cultures, being welcomed can be overwhelming. If you have ever been formally welcomed by a tribal culture, specifically one from the Pacific region, it is a loud, emotive experience. After the initial dance is over, it gets up close and personal with all notable chiefs pressing noses and foreheads together with the visitors. This is a full welcoming experience, and when it is completed, there is a sense that you are almost part of the tribe. The point of this ritual of welcoming someone into the tribe is to make them feel exactly that—at home.

Hospitality is big on God's list of Christian attributes. He even makes it a priority in determining who is fit to lead the church. Throughout the Old and New Testaments, God made it clear that we are to receive the stranger, care for those in need, and share our lives with others. You are an example to those you are showing hospitality to. Through you they can meet the Father. Consider friends that are on the fringe of your Christian circle and invite them into your home.

Father, help me to be hospitable. Help me to show others your heart for them.

IF PAUL CAN DO IT

A cheerful heart is a good medicine,
but a downcast spirit dries up the bones.
PROVERBS 17:22 NRSV

Have you ever spent time being with friends who do not do anything but complain? It is wearing on everyone listening to them. There is no joy in sitting with those who grumble about their life and whine about their circumstances. We have allowance for each other to go through dark times, and we want to be there for others as they would be for us, but once we are over a difficulty there is nothing more refreshing than spending time with someone who is positive. It brings healing to the soul.

Positivity comes from finding, in any circumstance, a reason to be thankful. It is not a matter for the fainthearted; it is easy to complain when a situation goes bad. What can we do differently? As Paul wrote in the verse above, it is important to be thankful in all things, and that enables a person to overcome extraordinary situations. It is likely that you have not been through what Paul experienced, yet he calls you to be thankful. If he can do it, so can you.

Jesus, help me to have a cheerful heart. I ask that you would help me be thankful in all that I am going through and to see you in every situation.

RENEWED

Do not conform to the pattern of this world, but be transformed by the renewing of your mind. Then you will be able to test and approve what God's will is— his good, pleasing and perfect will.

ROMANS 12:2 NIV

Have you watched the car shop shows where they take an old, beat-up vehicle and restore it? It is amazing to see how humans can restore things to look and feel new. What a gift that is. If you take this further, thinking about all the areas of restoration where we have an impact, it is incredible: nature, relationships, vitality, health, and all manner of manufactured items. If we who are not God can transform from bad to good in so many manners, what can God do? His renewal strategies are better. His mind is sharper. His vision is clearer. He is not limited.

When you read the verse above, how does the thought of God being the master at renewal impact you? Can he rehabilitate even the darkest of minds? Yes, he can. Transformation and renewal are part of what God can and will do in you.

Father, thank you for renewing my mind and making me a better disciple of Jesus. Help me to know and do your will.

A FIRM PATH

He lifted me out of the pit of despair,
out of the mud and the mire.
He set my feet on solid ground
and steadied me as I walked along.
PSALM 40:2 NIV

We have all seen those movies with a mud pit looming ahead and the character unknowingly stumbles into it while trying to escape multiple adversaries. Or the main characters are isolated, alone, and unable to save themselves. But in each case, it takes a savior; someone has to come along and rescue them from the mire. Those who were once desperate and overcome with fear are set free and set upon solid ground. What a feeling of gratitude and joy must be filling that person.

Jesus has done the same for you. Sometimes it may take you a moment to recall but you were helpless, stuck in your sin, and facing death. He came and rescued you and set your feet upon a firm path.

Jesus, thank you for giving me a firm path to walk on and for rescuing me from my sin. I confess that I am lost without you, and I need your salvation.

CONSIDERATE

We who are strong must be considerate of those who are sensitive
about things like this. We must not just please ourselves.
For even Christ didn't live to please himself.
ROMANS 15:1, 3 NLT

A thoughtful person is considerate of others, kind in word and action, and selfless. We can usually find several like this in our circles. Hopefully, we find many, as we enjoy being with people like this. These are not always people that we necessarily want to be like because they tend to be quiet and reflective. Those who are successful, who stand out in crowd, and who are generally more charismatic relate to others on a different level. They are typically strong personalities, forceful, loud, and maybe even self-promoting.

There is a balance of these traits reflected in Christ. At times he pleased the crowd, doing miracles, rebuking the Pharisees for their hypocrisy, and standing up for the poor and the defenseless. But there was also a caring, unselfish, quiet side to him. He comforted his disciples, taught children, and was crucified without retaliating. He was truly the perfect man and the righteous Son of God. Though you may not have complete understanding as Jesus has, you can aim to do the things he did in the way he did them. Ask the Holy Spirit to help you in your consideration of others.

Father, help me to be considerate of others and to look to their needs before I just go ahead and do my own thing. I want to care for them like you do.

PROVISION

God is able to bless you abundantly, so that in all things at all times, having all
that you need, you will abound in every good work.

2 CORINTHIANS 9:8 NLT

This verse provides us a with a two-fold picture of God's sustenance. Not only does he supply what we need for our daily living, but he also gives what we need to do good works. He provides for both our spiritual and our physical needs. He intends that we always look to him for everything that we need because he can provide it. Not only does he want to provide for us, but he wants to help us to accomplish his will that we would have all we need in order to do our work for him.

You can look to God for help with your provisions as well as for your calling. He will give you all that you need to accomplish his will and you can be confident that he will help you complete his work.

God, I want to do your will and walk with you, trusting that you will provide for me. Help me as I get older to stay close to you and rely upon you alone.

SHARE

"I will give you a new heart, and a new spirit I will put within you. And I will remove the heart of stone from your flesh and give you a heart of flesh."

EZEKIEL 36:26 ESV

When God created Adam, he did so from the earth. It was not the earth that had the power, but God's Word. So, when God says that he can take the hardest heart, a stone heart, and make it flesh, we can be confident that he can. We know friends and people around us who are resistant to God. It seems like they will never know him, but the truth is, God can turn them to himself in an instant. All he needs is for them to demonstrate some humility before him.

We cannot give up sharing with all people about the great God we serve. They must know of his mercy and compassion. Think of your friends and people you know who seem distant from God and pray for them. Ask the Holy Spirit to soften their hearts and bring them to a place of humility before him.

Holy Spirit, help me to know who to pray for. I know that you want all men to know God and you are filled with love and compassion for us all.

NO BLAME SHAME

Nothing in all creation is hidden from God. Everything is naked and exposed
before his eyes, and he is the one to whom we are accountable.
HEBREWS 4:13 NLT

Have you ever watched an animal that is wearing an unusual garment
or has something stuck to it? For instance, sometimes people will put
little boots or socks on their pet's feet. The animal will dance and jump
around, trying to get the strange items off. Until they feel free from it,
they can't seem to focus on anything else.

We are like that when it comes to being transparent. It is foreign to us.
We like to keep control over what we show and don't show other people.
Shame about the whole truth drives us this way. Like the animal when
it's wearing strange little boots, when we feel shame or we feel exposed,
we dance around, pointing fingers, lying, deceiving, and hiding. So often,
we will do anything to avoid being vulnerable. Ironically, God always
sees right through us. God loves you and wants you to be as vulnerable
as a child; to sit still on his lap, take comfort in knowing him, and let him
speak to you. No shame, just comfort.

*Father, help me to not point fingers and blame others. I want to take
responsibility for my actions, and I ask for your forgiveness where I have
not. Help me to know I am not ashamed before you.*

JUNE 11

ACTIVE IN THE WORD

*The word of God is living and active, and sharper than any two-edged sword,
even penetrating as far as the division of soul and spirit, of both joints and
marrow, and able to judge the thoughts and intentions of the heart.*
HEBREWS 4:12 NASB

Activity infers that something is alive: the ant scurrying around preparing for winter, the lion prowling at night, or the bees making honey. Perhaps for those who have read this verse before, it makes sense the that living and active tie together so well. However, when it comes to words and what we read on paper, how is that active? The answer is found in the source of the words themselves. It is the source that is actively making the Word of God alive. Jesus, the actual Word of God, works within us and in the world. He is active through his Word. This is why the Word is capable of judging the intentions of the heart. God is behind it.

This concept is explained in Matthew chapter five when Jesus encounters the centurion. The centurion believed that Jesus could simply speak, and his Word would be carried out because the centurion completely understood authority. There is no greater authority than the one who spoke the sun, the moon, and the stars into their very existence. Today, in your life, Jesus' Word is active. Take time to listen for it.

Father, open your Word up to me and help me to hear it and obey.

SECURITY BELONGS TO GOD

"Do not lay up for yourselves treasures on earth, where moth and rust destroy and where thieves break in and steal, but lay up for yourselves treasures in heaven, where neither moth nor rust destroys and where thieves do not break in and steal. For where your treasure is, there your heart will be also."

MATTHEW 6:19-21 ESV

The wind was picking up, so they headed home. They docked at the wharf. Tying off the boat, the youth turned, smiling at his new skill. He had learned it from his dad. It was not a hard knot, but if you didn't do it right it became a slip knot, and that would not be good for tying off a boat. They trudged off to the house, bummed that they did not catch more than a few fish. The afternoon passed by, and with the cool of the evening, the wind dropped. Time to head back out. They came around the bend. *Where was the boat?* Panic set in for both of them. Dad looked at him questioning, "Did you secure the boat?"

In this life where moth, rust, thieves, and harmful people seem to dominate, your security is found in God's eternal promises. Everything you have you will eventually be gone anyway. God is your only guarantee.

God, help me to trust in you. I pray that my life is not about what the world has to offer, which is worth nothing in the end. Help me to value relationships above all other things.

A SUN AND SHIELD

The LORD God is a sun and shield;
the LORD bestows favor and honor.
No good thing does he withhold from those who walk uprightly.
PSALM 84:11 ESV

There is great favor upon those who follow Christ. When we talk about following him, it is not like the typical western Christian. We are speaking of those who sacrifice the pleasures of this life to walk and talk like Jesus did. Jesus was no mediocre Jew. He stood out big time. He listened to the Father and did all that he commanded. Because of his devotion, he was attentive to the voice of the Holy Spirit.

We, too, as followers of Christ, are to be as devoted and focused. But life comes at us hard, and there is much to distract us. We have to be disciplined and desperate to walk as Jesus walked. Jesus set you free to choose how each day unfolds. You can follow him, or you can follow your own desires. He has given you strength and friends that can help you to follow him each day.

Jesus, I pray that you would be a shield for me, to protect me from following other gods. I want your favor and blessing so I can be like you.

GENUINE

I praise you, for I am fearfully and wonderfully made.
Wonderful are your works; my soul knows it very well.
PSALM 139:14 ESV

They were walking along the beach skipping stones across the smooth water. Five, nine, four, twelve! Father and son were having so much fun. Then they tossed some driftwood into the ocean and started bombing it. With both big and little stones, they tried to perfect the drop so a stone would land right on top of the floating wood. The son was impressed at his father's accuracy. He looked up at him with admiration: "I bet you are the best in the world at this, Dad." His father stopped mid launch, looked at his son, and with candor replied, "I am likely not the best at anything, son. There is always someone in the world more skilled than I am." He finished his throw, hitting the wood. The son pondered a moment and then, as if speaking for God, he replied, "You are the best at being you, Dad."

Being genuine or authentic means having an honest evaluation of yourself that develops into a full understanding. It comes as part of maturity. The father was being genuine about who he was. Your confidence is in your Creator and who he made you to be, not in acquiring the title of "best" at anything other than being yourself.

Father, help me to like myself as you do. You know the mature person that I will be, and I ask that you would help me get there.

FOUND

David danced before the LORD with all his might, wearing a priestly garment.
David and all the people of Israel brought up the Ark of the LORD with shouts of
joy and the blowing of rams' horns.

2 SAMUEL 6:14-15 NLT

His buddy messaged him to hang out, and in his distraction, he ran off
and put the remote down in a random place. When he came home, he
wanted to jump online. A new map was being released and it was time
to kick some butt. He searched everywhere. Panic started to set in as
time drew near. He started yelling at his dog, his siblings, and even at his
mom. But then he found it! He was over the moon. Happiness replaced
sadness. He got on and laughed with his friends about it. And, yes, they
destroyed their opponents.

It's a minor comparison to what David experienced bringing the ark
home. The ark was lost to an enemy for a long time. Yet, you understand
the joy of finding something you lost. God has this same joy over you
when you turn to him even when you have sinned. He wants you to
always come back to him.

*God, I know my heart wanders from you. Help me to always come back to
you.*

POWER IN WORDS

The tongue has the power of life and death,
and those who love it will eat its fruit.
PROVERBS 18:21 ESV

What we speak has power. When God created the earth, he spoke it into being. He didn't think it or use his hands. He spoke. We can also speak blessing or cursing over our lives and the lives of others. If we practice speaking positively with words of encouragement and gratitude, our lives are blessed. Without a doubt, those who live like this are happier. Depression and sadness surround those who complain, gossip, and slander others. Their lives are miserable.

As you go about your days, practice the power of gratitude. Even in your troubled times find things to be thankful for and remind yourself of the promises you have in Christ. You will find that God reminds you of his presence and will empower you to overcome all your trials.

Father, thank you for the power of words in my life. Help me to read your promises aloud and believe in them. Teach me how to be thankful even in my most difficult times.

ALERT

Going a little farther, he fell with his face to the ground and prayed, "My Father, if it is possible, may this cup be taken from me. Yet not as I will, but as you will." Then he returned to his disciples and found them sleeping. "Couldn't you men keep watch with me for one hour?" he asked Peter. "Watch and pray so that you will not fall into temptation. The spirit is willing, but the flesh is weak."

MATTHEW 26:38-41 ESV

When Jesus was going through this difficult time, the disciples seemed to be ignorant of his trouble. They had just enjoyed a great supper with him, they had seen his great miracles, and they were likely excited about Jesus becoming the new king of Israel. When he said to keep watch, they were relaxing which is probably why they fell asleep. They didn't understand the context of the circumstances in which they were living.

You, also, can get sleepy, not realizing what God is doing around you. Ask him to help you stay awake, to be alert, and to partner with him in what he is doing. You are important to his kingdom.

Jesus, help me to partner with you in doing your will on earth. Keep me alert and awake so that I can pray and know your will. I know I will often fail, but you can strengthen me.

JUNE 18

SENSITIVE

"Where have you laid him?" he asked.
"Come and see, Lord," they replied.
Jesus wept. Then the Jews said, "See how he loved him!"
JOHN 11:34-36 NIV

Sensitivity is not always a characteristic that we think of as manly. However, it can show up in different forms. Christ was sensitive and perceptive. He wasn't delicate, which is what we may consider equal to the word *sensitive*. He was searching, understanding, considerate, and caring. His sensitivity had nothing to do with a weakened self-perception. He was a strong man who was not afraid of being sensitive.

As you mature, you will also find that you can afford to be caring and concerned for others' wellbeing. You are able to look beyond yourself and show thoughtfulness in such a way that you may have previously considered weakness. Sensitivity is also important when it comes to hearing the moving of the Holy Spirit. He speaks to you when you listen carefully.

Holy Spirit, I want to hear you speak. Jesus, help me to have open ears to what your Spirit is saying.

ASSURED

We know that in all things God works for the good of those who love him,
who have been called according to his purpose.

ROMANS 8:28 NIV

What keeps you going in life? Is it certainty, creativity, or chaos? God
knew when he created us that mankind would fall. He knew that he was
going to have to save us. He had a plan and a purpose for us. His exciting
goal, and his ultimate purpose was to have a people of his own creation
who loved him wholeheartedly and who lived with him in his creation.

This is certain; God will have what he wants. His plan is perfect, and his
will for us is to be included in this end plan. With him we have certainty
and creativity that overcomes chaos. Your life is not dull with God, but it
is defined and certain. You are not unsure but assured. Your life is in his
hands.

*Jesus, thank you for giving me your promises. Help me to believe in them to
the point where my life is devoted to you as you are to me.*

CAPTIVATING

One thing I ask from the LORD, this only do I seek:
that I may dwell in the house of the LORD all the days of my life,
to gaze on the beauty of the LORD and to seek him in his temple.

PSALM 27:4 NIV

When the word *captivating* comes to mind, what do you think about?
Do you have visions of a pretty girl, a spectacular sunset, a range of
mysterious mountains, a fantastic film, a beautiful beach, or perhaps
melodic music? God placed within us a desire to be captivated. We are
a people filled with hunger for pleasurable experiences. This was not a
mistake on God's part, nor is it evil. His intention for us is that we are
intrigued by him, and in finding him we experience true joy and delight.
When we connect with his Holy Spirit, there is nothing more captivating.
We may not allow ourselves enough time, but if we do, we will find that
the creator of desire is actually the best answer to fulfilling the craving.

You can get back to a place where you are captivated by Jesus. Sit at his
feet and allow his Spirit to fill you afresh. Wait upon him.

*Holy Spirit, help me to be patient and please connect me with Jesus. I want
to experience all that he has for me. I want to delight in him.*

DIGGING FOR GOLD

All the ways of a person are clean in his own sight,
But the LORD examines the motives.
PROVERBS 16:2 NASB

Determining what motivates us can be like digging for gold. If you have ever watched gold miners at work, it takes some hard labor and experience. It's usually a sacrifice, but it gives great rewards. If you know what motivates you, going after it will give you passion, joy, and a reason to live.

One of the top motivators for males is to have a sense of accomplishment. If a goal is set and completed, there is a release of hormones called endorphins that bring us pleasure. When days passively drift by, we can feel aimless and pointless. You have a purpose. God very much wants you to be motivated to seek him. In finding him, you will receive joy. He aligns this purpose of his with roles and tasks that you will fulfil. He wants you to experience motivation for life!

Father, I don't want to waste my life on things that don't matter to your kingdom. Help me to be motivated by godly things and not by riches or pleasure.

ELDER HONOR

A fool despises his father's instruction,
but whoever heeds reproof is prudent.
PROVERBS 15:5 ESV

How many of us think our parents know what they are talking about?
They don't know what we experience, do they? When they were teens,
life was so different. Did they experience similar emotions and changes
in their lives? They probably did. So, when they speak about life and
instructions on how to live, they are talking from valuable experience.
They have learned and survived. If we want to be wise, we should listen
to what they say and understand how to apply it to our lives.

If you want to walk in a pleasing manner before God, humility must
be a foundation. One way to show that is by learning from your elders.
Listening to them and trying to understand how their perspective can
apply to your life now is wisdom.

*God, help me to learn from my elders and to listen to them. I want to honor
my parents and I need your help to do so.*

REFRESHING

Repent and return, so that your sins may be wiped away,
in order that times of refreshing may come from the presence of the Lord.

ACTS 3:19 NASB

There is a time when you are working in the hot sun when it becomes unbearable. Your shirt is drenched, you are covered in dirt, and the air is thick. It saps your energy quickly, and if you don't consume a certain amount of liquid, you can become dehydrated, dizzy, and eventually even lose consciousness. When a cool breeze starts blowing, it feels luxurious. It is so refreshing especially if paired with a splash of fresh water from a hose. A small reprieve from the heat, and you are ready to work again.

This is what God wants for us. Our lives, though full of good things, can also be troublesome. We are in a battle, worn down and tired, but he comes to us like a fresh breeze and a drink of cool water. He gives us renewed strength to continue the fight. Are you weary from fighting sin? Sit and wait on God. Let his forgiveness refresh you and give you a new sense of strength. He does not shame you as you seek him.

God, I come to you weary and tired. Thank you for your forgiveness. Refresh me. I need you.

FERVENT

In your relationships with one another, have the same mindset as Christ Jesus:
Who, being in very nature God, did not consider equality with God something
to be used to his own advantage; rather, he made himself nothing by taking the
very nature of a servant, being made in human likeness…he humbled himself by
becoming obedient to death.

PHILIPPIANS 2:5-8 NIV

He was ready. His weapon of choice was the same as the others'. Their
bodies were tense with anticipation. In his mind, he pictured the attack.
This strike would be most efficient, that one would deliver the most
powerful damage, and one other would make the final blow. Ready, set,
go! He picked up the axe and enthusiastically swung it overhead. *Chop.*
And again. *Chop.* With intensity, he swung that axe time after time. "We
have a winner!" He had won; he was elated. Someone congratulated
him, and another pointed out the blood on his hand. In his zeal, a small
splinter had flown off and stuck him. Ah, a bloodied warrior. He proudly
pulled out the sliver of wood.

Jesus took on death and was bloodied well beyond this log-splitting
competitor. He was determined. He didn't compare himself. He didn't
do it for fame or competition. He did it to win and his prize was us, his
glorious church.

*Jesus, help me to sacrifice for others as you did for me. I need your help to
fight against my own desires so that I can serve others well.*

SHARPENED

As iron sharpens iron,
so people can improve each other.
PROVERBS 27:17 NCV

We look to enrich our lives on many fronts. It is all about advertising that inundates our lives: make your life better by adding this, that, and another thing! We have even enriched our most basic nutrients down to the most critical of components—water. Now you have to choose what water to buy. It seems that our culture has developed an enrichment complex. At the core of this marketing mindset, is the message that says that life is not enough as it is, so you need to add more. However, the reality is that our lives have become so full that we have become dull to the good things that God has already given us, such as the people around us.

If we want our lives to be enriched, then we should fill it up with good relationships: those that cause us to grow and mature by intentional sharpening.

You have friends who encourage you to follow God, and others who entice you to do things God does not approve of. Hang out with those who follow Jesus and will challenge you to do the same.

Jesus, help me to be with friends who challenge me to love you better. Protect me from those who take me away from you. Guide me in choosing my friends.

CORE ELEMENTS

"The glory that you have given me I have given to them, that they may be one even as we are one, I in them and you in me, that they may become perfectly one, so that the world may know that you sent me and loved them even as you loved me."

JOHN 17:22-23 ESV

Jesus is speaking a blessing over his church, a prayer that he continues to pray over us today. He desires for us to be united, yet when you look around the world, the church is fragmented by many different opinions about Scripture. What is it going to take to bring us together? The only answer to unity in the church is a movement of the Holy Spirit which overcomes all men and bring us to a place of wholeness like we have never seen before. Jesus' words will come true. Before he returns, his church, his bride, will be unified and desperate for him. We will be a church that is passionate about the gospel and the return of our Savior.

It is important as a believer to understand that some elements of your faith are absolutely critical, and those core elements will be shared in the Word of God as well as by all true believers. Pray for God to bring the church together and for his Holy Spirit to be poured out upon it.

Father, please pour your Spirit out on the church. Help me to understand what is critical in my faith to believe and to fight for.

NOT HOLDING OFFENSE

As high as the heavens are above the earth,
so great is his love for those who fear him;
as far as the east is from the west,
so far has he removed our transgressions from us.

PSALM 103:11-12 NIV

What does it take to forgive someone? A lot. It is not about putting something on a shelf and forgetting about it or releasing it to the wind. Forgiveness is about choosing not to hold on to the offense. That is what God does. He doesn't sit and recount our sins. That would be awful. Who could count their sins against God? As he forgives us, so he asks us to forgive others. We choose not to remember what they have done against us.

This is hard when we really want justice. We have feelings, thoughts, and even scars. How do we choose not to remember these offenses when we experience something that triggers a past hurt? Like Christ, you have to put your hope in the one who judges justly. He will make things right one day. In the meantime, practice forgiving those who have hurt you by not dwelling on all the wrong they have done.

Jesus, as you have forgiven me, help me to forgive others who have wronged me.

DEPENDENT

Each time he said, "My grace is all you need. My power works best in weakness."
So now I am glad to boast about my weaknesses, so that the power of Christ can
work through me.

2 CORINTHIANS 12:9 ESV

Males do not like to be weak, and not just in physical strength either.
We do not like to be seen as weak in intelligence, emotion, ability, etc.
Anything that seems less when compared to others. We fight it all the
time. Yet here Paul says that he embraces weakness, that in being weak
he is strengthened by Christ. Ironically, the weakness that the world
shames is the one that God embraces. He takes those dependent on him
and uses them the most for his purposes. He resists the pride of man and
their need to be strong, and he gives strength to those who know they are
weak and come to him for their strength.

As you gain understanding of God's upside-down-inside-out kingdom,
you will notice how he honors humility above many other virtues.
Practice it by recognizing and accepting your inability to do all things
and your dependence on him.

You are right, God. I am weak, but you are strong. Help me to depend on
you and to be real about my own abilities and strengths.

GOODNESS, JUSTICE, PROTECTION

Your goodness is as high as the mountains.
Your justice is as deep as the great ocean.
LORD, you protect both people and animals.

PSALM 36:6 NCV

Who doesn't love a good movie with justice being served in the end? We dislike it when the bad guy gets away with the crime. This concept of righteousness has been in humanity since the beginning. We long for things to be made right, especially when we are personally involved. Oddly enough, if we are the one doing wrong, we want to be shown mercy when we are caught. We like the idea of getting away with it. What wicked people we are!

We want justice but we also want to avoid punishment for the things we do against others. Thank God that he is a gracious and righteous judge! Jesus reminds you that you will be judged by the manner in which you judge others. He is asking you to give grace to others if you want to receive his grace. So, when your family or friends offend you, be gracious and respond with kindness. He will reward this.

Jesus, help me to be gracious to those who offend me. I want to be more like you in my responses to others.

UNFAILING

The Lord is not slow in keeping his promise, as some understand slowness. Instead he is patient with you, not wanting anyone to perish, but everyone to come to repentance.

2 PETER 3:9 NIV

Jesus is a man of his Word. He keeps his promises. He never fails, he has never failed, and he will never fail. Have you ever browsed a list of words that describe core fears? Often men pick failure. We are afraid to fail. It starts as young boys and carries through our teenage years. Because of this known fear in men, research on vulnerability has grown. It was found that men are afraid of vulnerability because in being so, they may be labeled as weak. Of all the things men do not want to be, "weak" ranks high on the list.

Jesus never fails. He just doesn't. You can be like him, but you are not him. You are going to fail; your promises are not as sure as his are. His assurance is trustworthy. His Word is a guarantee. He will complete what he says he will do in you. Trust in him.

Thank you that you keep your promises, God. Help me to do the same. Even though I am not perfect, and I will fail, I want to walk as closely to you as I can.

FAITH IS A KEY

Since we have been justified by faith,
we have peace with God through our Lord Jesus Christ.
ROMANS 5:1 NIV

Faith is the key to Christianity. A key unlocks a door and gives access to whatever is inside. Faith allows for salvation and that gives us access to all the blessings and responsibilities that God has for us. Without it, we do not have access to God's promises. Without it, we do works and ineffectively attempt to gain our own salvation. And without faith, our continued sanctification cannot take place. It is important then that we foster faith within ourselves and within our communities.

How do you build faith? You share a godly life, you encourage others in your experiences with him, and you spend time together in God's Word and in worship. As you do these things, you recognize his involvement in your life. It builds trust in his character and gives assurance that he is actively working in you.

I believe in you, Jesus. Help me in my faith. Help me to believe and to share with my friends and family my experience of you.

COURTEOUS

Let us consider how to stir up one another
to love and good works.
HEBREWS 10:24 ESV

When you encounter a rude person, what is your first response?
Usually, we don't respond well and often not in a civil manner. It takes a
disciplined person to answer well to someone who is rude. God wants us
to learn how to control our responses and to be polite even when we are
not receiving a similar courtesy.

How refreshing it is when we meet someone who is well-mannered and
considerate. These people are a delight to be with and often speak with
gentleness that gives rise to good conversation. To be courteous, we have
to learn how to lay aside our preferences and serve others. This could be
something that our parents instilled in us early in life, or we can learn
it now. It is never too late for you to start considering others! A starting
point could be as small as opening doors for your friends and family as
often as you have the chance. Help them carry something, or just look for
simple ways to serve.

*Jesus, help me to be considerate of others. Show me their needs so that I can
be like you and assist them*

IMAGINE

What no eye has seen, nor ear heard, nor the heart of man imagined,
what God has prepared for those who love him.
1 CORINTHIANS 2:9 ESV

Imagine you are at a cabin with your family. Step outside and feel the warmth of the sun hitting your face. Breathe in deeply and let the fresh air fill your lungs. Smell the different fragrances in the air and hear the pleasant sounds of animals as they actively go about their day. This is just a small snapshot of the beauty that God has made, and we get to enjoy now. Yet we do not see or hear as we will when we are resurrected.

The Bible makes it clear that what we experience on earth pales in comparison to what he has for us in eternity. Prophets try to describe what they see in heaven with words, but it does not do it justice. God has incredible things for us to experience and we should be excited about our future in him. Take time to read your Bible and find Scriptures that describe God and the heavens. Imagine a place where the beauty of our world is combined with the majesty of heaven. God has things in store for you far beyond your greatest dreams.

Father, show me your creativeness and let me experience some of what you are preparing me for. I want to be excited about my future in you.

CLEANSED AND FORGIVEN

If we confess our sins, He is faithful and just to forgive us our sins and to cleanse us from all unrighteousness.

1 JOHN 1:9 NKJV

Without realizing it, we may be subconsciously trying to appease God when we sin. We might do this by trying to be nice to people, kinder and more caring than normal, and thinking that it will matter to God. It does, but not to earn our forgiveness. Sometimes we react the other way around by hardening our hearts and wanting nothing to do with him for a while. We might think that if we sin more and ignore the Holy Spirit now, maybe we can come back to him later when we will be ready to truly stop sinning.

What we don't realize when we do this is that Jesus does not ask us to *prove* anything. He doesn't require anything from us. He already paid the price for our sin. He just asks that we humble ourselves, repent of our sins, and turn to him. Again, and again. And again, and again. Each time, he is faithful, and he will forgive us. Each time, he is just. He paid in his own blood and his own death in order for us to be forgiven. He cleanses us from all sin.

Jesus, thank you for your forgiveness. I know I do not deserve your mercy and kindness, yet you give it to me. Help me to keep short accounts with you and to repent of my sin quickly.

DETERMINED

The God of all grace, who called you to his eternal glory in Christ,
after you have suffered a little while, will himself restore you
and make you strong, firm and steadfast.

1 PETER 5:10 NIV

He was young for the trip but old enough to do it. He loved adventure and a challenge. It set something off in his heart that made him feel truly alive. On this adventure, things had started well and then slowly deteriorated. The first night was great, but his arm was sore from paddling since they had to go such a long distance that morning. He remembered hurting it at pole vaulting practice earlier in the month, but he labored on. Every stroke felt like multiple needle-pokes in his arm. After several hours and multiple portages with backpacks, it was not improving. He resolved to make it without complaining, but the pain was more consistent than he was. A quick word was mentioned, he popped a few pain killers, and the pain dissipated. Why had he been so stubborn? Why didn't he just seek help earlier?

There are positive and negative aspects to all strengths and God wants yours to be submitted to him. Bring your determination to him and ask him to help you.

Help me, Jesus, to be dependent on you even with the gifts and strengths you have given me.

DELIGHT

Delight yourself in the LORD,
and he will give you the desires of your heart.
PSALM 37:4 ESV

There is a saying, "You are what you eat," which, when you think about it, seems rather gross. You may have eaten fried chicken feet, balut, or raw seaweed with mushy fish and noodles. So, what are you then? When not taken literally, the saying simply implies that if you eat good food, you will be healthy. Eat bad food, and you will be unhealthy. There is also a correlation to this statement and the verse above. When we delight in something, we pursue it. We consume it. We want it. God made us to enjoy things. It was the original design in creation that was destroyed by sin.

Instead of pursuing lesser delights, if you delight in God, he doubles down on it for you and gives you new and healthy desires. When you are delighting in God, those desires in your heart are from him. You then pursue what you delight in.

Father, I want to learn to delight in you. Help me to remember your Word, to follow your ways, and to obey your voice.

TRUE TRANSPARENCY

I resolved to know nothing while I was with you except Jesus Christ and him crucified. I came to you in weakness and fear, and with much trembling.

1 CORINTHIANS 2:2-3 NIV

A new wave has crashed our society into change. We're not looking for leaders who are experts and who have it all together. We want leaders who are authentic. It is hard for leaders who have been trained for generations to demonstrate other traits such as teachability, self-control, and authority. But so much failure of these same leaders has led to a generation crying out for authenticity. We want to see mistakes and learn from them. We want work together and learn together with our leaders, and therefore be inspired by them. It is a shift that enables more transparency, but it has also loosened morality. We are broken people, and our leadership is doomed to failure.

Jesus was authentic. He was sincere, realistic, faithful, and trustworthy. We can sharpen who we are by following his example and living in the same manner. You can be authentic by not living to please others, but instead by living to show others the love and goodness of God in how he made you. Be you, but love as Christ.

Jesus, show me how to love others in the way that you made me to do. I am uniquely made by you.

PRACTICING FOR THE WIN

Do you not know that in a race all the runners run, but only one gets the prize? Run in such a way as to get the prize. Everyone who competes in the games goes into strict training. They do it to get a crown that will not last, but we do it to get a crown that will last forever.

1 CORINTHIANS 9:24-25 NIV

Almost every child has run a race. When we do, we usually size up our competition, and start to self-talk; "I can beat that guy!" "Ooh, not sure if I can take him." We naturally want to win, but we know quickly how to evaluate the winners. We can recognize a practiced athlete. The kid that plays basketball and football is likely the one to win. The rest of us running, and who casually play sports will try, but really the guy who does this all the time will win.

This is what Paul's point is in this verse. You will win if you live your life with discipline and training. You need habit, repetition, and re-dos. Do it again. Practice prayer, practice reading your Bible, practice being with other believers. Make it a habit and you will win the prize.

Jesus, I need you to give me the strength to be disciplined. Help me learn the habit of seeking you.

JULY 9

STRONG

*I pray that from his glorious, unlimited resources he will empower you
with inner strength through his Spirit.*
EPHESIANS 3:16 NLT

From his demeanor you would not have realized he only had one arm. He carried himself with dignity and power. His strength was not lacking. When he set to a task, he carried it out effectively like any full-bodied person. He could pick up a hundred pounds in one arm and carry it without showing strain. His family was killed in the same accident that caused him to lose his arm, but the scars on his heart were much deeper. Still, he remained steadfast in Christ, knowing that he would see them again. His closeness to his Savior gave him the strength and hope that he needed each day to remain resilient in the face of the worst pain—the loss of his loved ones.

When you face hard times, God has unlimited comfort that will strengthen you. He will surround you with angels to give you daily encouragement. He will pour out his Spirit upon you so you will not thirst or hunger for anything. His love will be yours like you have never known. That is what will make you strong. Trust in his empowering grace.

God, comfort me in my trouble. I want to trust in you even in my most difficult days. Show me your love and power so that I can be strengthened by you.

INNOCENT OF EVIL

Prove yourselves to be blameless and innocent, children of God above reproach
in the midst of a crooked and perverse generation, among whom you appear as
lights in the world.
PHILIPPIANS 2:15 NASB

In Cabo San Lucas, when the sun is shining and the surf is small, you
can look down into the water and see lots of gold flecks. It shimmers as it
catches the light. It almost feels like you are swimming in gold dust. We
are intrigued by brilliant things. If a shiny object catches our attention,
we immediately start to wonder what it is. If we can pick it up, we marvel
at the reflection of light especially if it reveals beautiful changing colors.
The same wonderment comes upon us at night as we gaze at vividly
shining stars contrasted by the dark sky.

You are like one of these stars to Jesus. He looks down upon the
earth and sees you shining for him. The Father takes delight in seeing
your brightness against the surrounding darkness. He knows how to
strengthen you and to give you boldness to shine brightly for him.

*Father, teach me how to be innocent of evil and to show those around me
what it looks like to be a disciple of Jesus. I want to be a good witness to the
rest of the world.*

INTELLIGENT

Until we all attain to the unity of the faith and of the knowledge of the Son of God, to mature manhood, to the measure of the stature of the fullness of Christ.
EPHESIANS 4:13 ESV

There are many types of intelligence as defined in the study of human development. It's standard in the field to list nine: logical- mathematical, linguistic, musical, naturalist, existential, interpersonal, kinesthetic, intra-personal, and spatial. In our western society, we often value people who demonstrate a narrow band of these, but we miss out on seeing the gifted areas of knowledge in others. Not until we need them, do we appreciate what they have.

Have you ever been lost in the woods and one of your friends seems to easily find their way out? Or you're relaxing with friends and one of them picks up a guitar and fills the room with music? Or another relates to everybody in the group with ease and empathizes naturally? These are examples of the beauty and diversity of intelligence that God has placed among us. It is God's intention that you rely on others for their strengths, and you share with them yours. It is his intention that no one man has it all together, but that all men together have it.

God, I want to be independent, but I know that is not how you made me. Help me to appreciate and embrace the strengths of others.

FORTHRIGHT

Having put away falsehood, let each one of you speak the truth
with his neighbor, for we are members one of another.
EPHESIANS 4:25 ESV

If you have ever lived in the Midwest, you will know people who won't tell you how they really feel. Being straight forward isn't something that comes naturally there. Contrast that with people on the East Coast who speak openly. They both need a little of what the other has! To that point, there is balance in life that we must have when we have relationships with people.

Being forthright is important and valuable, but as with all things, it must be tempered with love. A good approach when sharing a point is to first understand where the other person is coming from. Then without judgment and with humility, express your view with confidence.

Father, you are true and right, and I admit I have a lot to learn. Help me to speak truth, but also to listen and love well.

COMFORT

The LORD himself goes before you and will be with you;
he will never leave you nor forsake you.
Do not be afraid; do not be discouraged.

DEUTERONOMY 31:8 NIV

There is great comfort in knowing that things are certain. Not only is it comforting, but it also reduces anxiety. We have way too much anxiety in our world. In between the stress of school, work, family, and social media, we are somehow meant to relax and find peace. It does not come easily, so we can be particularly grateful for those certain big things like having a home to come back to and a bed upon which to lay our head. Consistency and regular habits bring about a sense of security that we need in this crazy life. This is where God promises to be there. He is always around. He is committed to us.

In your times of stress, ask God to come and remind you of his consistent care. He wants you to turn to him and ask for his help.

God, I admit that I am stressed and anxious. Help me to find comfort in you. I want to trust you and to seek you at all times.

SHOW ME PRIDE

Always be humble and gentle.
Be patient with each other,
making allowance for each other's faults
because of your love.

EPHESIANS 4:2 NLT

It is the humble who promote peace and act with patience. They keep unity and this goes a long way in demonstrating love. Who among us can truly say that they are humble? Wouldn't that in itself deny humility? In his autobiography, Benjamin Franklin wrote about thirteen virtues that lead to humility: temperance, silence, order, resolution, frugality, industry, sincerity, justice, moderation, cleanliness, tranquility, and chastity. He practiced these but found, frustratingly, that he ended up becoming prideful of his accomplishment as he established each virtue, thus undoing his goal!

In you there is pride that is difficult to unravel. Even if you speak lowly of yourself, there is pride. Pride hides. The only antidote is to be filled with the Holy Spirit and practice his fruit. Out of this practice he will operate on your heart and show you your pride. This is by no means fun, but it is beneficial for his kingdom!

Holy Spirit, show me my pride and help me to be a humble person. I want your love to fill my heart.

CHOSEN

You are a chosen people, a royal priesthood, a holy nation, God's special possession, that you may declare the praises of him who called you out of darkness into his wonderful light.

1 PETER 2:9 NIV

God has chosen us. We don't know how, and we don't know why. We wonder about why we were chosen because we think that if we could know, perhaps it would give us more understanding about ourselves or our value. But in reality, it is not about us or that he chose us specifically. It is about him. He is holy, and wonderful, and merciful, and great. That is why we are to tell others about him.

You were set apart not because of yourself, but because he consecrated you based on who he is. He calls you to act accordingly: to be holy as he is holy. Continue each day to set yourself apart from the world. Strive to not love the world and to devote your heart to God.

God, thank you for choosing me for your purposes. Give me your eyes to see others as you do and to value them like you value me.

WORSHIP

Sing to him, sing praise to him;
tell of all his wonderful acts.
1 CHRONICLES 16:9 NIV

If you have ever enjoyed music to the point where you experience large emotions, then you will understand what it means to be moved by what you hear. We may not perceive it, but nearly every movie we watch that we have labelled as excellent has effective music. In fact, if you watch the same movie without its music, you likely will not have the same experience. It would appear less enticing and would definitely lack the same feelings. Next time you watch a movie, take note of what you are feeling as well as what you are hearing. Mute some of the scenes and you will be engaged mentally, but you will not be moved nearly as much.

Worship that engages music opens your heart to God. You are moved to connect with him in ways that you would not do otherwise. Often Scripture is brought into music because it moved someone, and they began to extol God and sing to him. Practice reading Scripture and find out if it moves you to praise God.

God, fill my heart with praise and worship. I want to experience your glory and be filled with joy in your presence.

IN TIMES OF TROUBLE

We also glory in tribulations, knowing that tribulation produces perseverance;
and perseverance, character; and character, hope.

ROMANS 5:3-4 NKJV

One foot in front of the other. That's what he had to do in order to keep going. If he was going to make it through, he had to be stubbornly resolute. "I am not going to stop moving." His commission was clear; if he did not get the message across, men would die. Through enemy ground, injury, and loss, he tirelessly trudged on. There was no one else to do this; he had to endure, and he could not stop. Many of us have not faced war, and we are very thankful to those who have. They learned an endurance through trials that we have not yet had to face. They paid a price that provided us with our freedom.

In your times of trouble, it is helpful to gain perspective. Are you bleeding? Are you stressed to the point of death? Do you live in a safe home with good things around you? This doesn't reduce what you feel, but it does remind you of a healthy perspective.

God, thank you for the good things in my life. In my trouble, remind me of your promises and guide me to those who can help me.

PURSUIT

"What good will it be for someone to gain the whole world, yet forfeit their soul?
Or what can anyone give in exchange for their soul?"
MATTHEW 16:26 NIV

It is easy for us to love the world. There are a lot of entertaining things in it that keep our minds captivated. There is also some really cool stuff to have; there's lots of new technology that makes life easy, transports us with little work, and keeps us constantly connected to the world. We love it and we want more.

Jesus is letting us know that if we work hard, we can gain all that stuff. We can actually get it all, but to what end? If we chase all the great stuff the world offers, we will find that in gaining it we have lost our souls. The person Jesus made us to be and the things he wants us to do will be set aside for the pursuit of stuff. Yuck. Let's make sure we are chasing after God and his kingdom. What he has for us is way better than anything human minds can make up.

Jesus, you were right, and I don't want my life to be about the pursuit of the world. I want my soul to be safe in you and I want my purpose to be directed by you.

DIRECTED

"Be strong and courageous, and act; do not fear nor be dismayed, for the LORD God, my God, is with you. He will not fail you nor forsake you until all the work for the service of the house of the LORD is finished."

1 CHRONICLES 28:20 NASB

God is intentional in what he does. He doesn't waste energy. He is efficient. When he puts it on our hearts to achieve something, he promises to be there and to see it through to completion. Sometimes we may feel like he's not with us especially if we face difficulties or someone is resisting us. But he is with us. His promise to not leave does not mean that he will always be visible. We have to seek him out in our troubled times, and he will reveal himself. It's not that he is playing hide- and-seek. He wants us to long for him and to choose him.

Think of how easy it is for us to be distracted. In a way, he stays back and invites us to set aside distractions so that we find him. He likes us to choose him. You never need to fear or fail to decide because you are afraid. Commit your way to God, ask him to guide you, and trust that he will direct your path.

I ask that you would direct my path, God. I commit my ways to you and trust in your leadership.

LEARN

If any of you lacks wisdom, you should ask God,
who gives generously to all without finding fault, and it will be given to you.

JAMES 1:5 NIV

Wisdom is different than knowledge. Wisdom includes knowledge and the ability to apply it well to every-day life. A wise person knows about life, has experience in it, continues to learn from it, and is able to make the correct responsive changes. They talk about learning, constantly identifying things they did not know, and pressing into God in order to understand more. It is the wise person who asks God for answers and who says to the Holy Spirit, "I don't know, but I want to learn more. Show me your ways and help me to understand life."

Those who are not wise do not listen to the Holy Spirit. They resist the wisdom of their elders; they speak as if they know the best choices already. They are not teachable. The Holy Spirit is in you and is with you to teach and guide you. Stop and listen. Read the Bible and ask for wisdom. Be a learner.

Holy Spirit, I don't know, and I want to learn more. Show me your ways and help me to understand life.

NEW HEIGHTS

Never be lacking in zeal,
but keep your spiritual fervor,
serving the Lord.
ROMANS 12:11 NIV

After resting a little from his fifth ride up, he drifted down effortlessly. He was exhausted from pedaling, but he was obsessed. This was the third day he had been doing this. As he rounded the corner, he saw the jump. His heart picked up pace as his bike slowed. Could he really do this? He was eager to show the boys how far he could go, perhaps even pulling off a small trick before landing. He was so intently focused that time seemed to stand still. Now he was only feet away and he began to frantically pedal in order to make up for his earlier hesitation. He was committed.

Woosh! He flew up and over the pile. He heard the exclamations from those watching, and euphoria embraced him as he became weightless. He imagined himself as a bird; he must have beaten the other records by now. Being pulled down quickly by gravity, he crashed to the earth. Laughter erupted as he scrambled along the ground. "What happened?" He stood there holding only his handlebars. His bike was irreparably broken, but he had beaten the record, and that was all that mattered to him in that moment.

God, like this boy, help me to pedal quickly after you. I want to experience new heights in my walk with you.

KIND OF LOVE

He has given us this command:
Anyone who loves God must also love their brother and sister.

1 JOHN 4:21 NIV

Who is your mother, father, brother, and sister? Jesus asked this question of the disciples. The answer was that those who seek to do the will of God are your family Anyone we know who seeks God and loves him as best they can are the ones we are to love well. Jesus encourages this on purpose, because in our world, people love themselves. They want their opinion to be heard. They want to express themselves and be known. Their lives revolve around themselves. But Jesus demands that we live differently. He wants us to be known for our love toward each other. He wants a people who serve each other, can see the needs of others, and then helps them. He said that if we love each other this way, men will see this and glorify God. They will also be saved.

Which of your friends seek to find God's will and then obey him? Call them up today, visit them, and encourage them. Do something kind for them. Perhaps it is one of your siblings or your parents. It applies to them too. Love them well and find ways to serve them.

Jesus, show me those I can love well, so that others will see you and want to know you.

BELIEF

Then Jesus told his disciples, "If anyone would come after me,
let him deny himself and take up his cross and follow me."
MATTHEW 16:24 ESV

We all have people we believe in or answers to many of life's questions
without thinking too hard. We believe that these are the best answers.
But when you ask someone what the meaning of life is and what
happens after you die, you often receive vague responses that require
further clarification. When we believe in something, we are certain of its
outcome. We trust that what we articulate is accurate.

That is what belief is all about: having conviction in the truth of a matter
and living your life in alignment with that truth. You believe in Jesus, that
he is God, that he is also human, and that he died, was buried, and was
resurrected for your salvation. He saved you, and he loves you.

*Jesus, I believe in you, and I lay down my life to follow you. Help me to do
this for the rest of my life.*

WATCHFUL

Be alert. Continue strong in the faith.
Have courage, and be strong. Do everything in love.
1 CORINTHIANS 16:13-14 NCV

They were in a foreign country. His parents left him with his little brother and took his older siblings. He was jealous. It wasn't fair that he had to stay with the brat. After they had been gone for well over an hour, the little brother started to get upset. The boy couldn't stand it anymore; he had been as vigilant as he could be. Now he needed out. He told the three-year-old boy to stay. He had no idea about the dangers of leaving a young child in a camper alone.

Adults realize a compromised situation where danger lurks, and they are on high alert for those situations. They learn this as their brains develop abilities to think differently, more maturely. They also learn awareness through life's lessons. These are qualities that children and adolescents do not have. You are growing in your understanding of the dangers on this earth. Also, as you grow spiritually, you will be more aware of what is happening around you. Satan wants you to be sleepy and indifferent. Jesus wants you to be sharp and ready.

Jesus, help me to be ready. I want my heart and mind to be prepared for your return.

EFFICIENT

Do you see a man skillful in his work?
He will stand before kings;
he will not stand before obscure men.

PROVERBS 22:29 ESV

As an administrative soul, he could see the most effective way of running a process so it was completed efficiently and with excellence. Lay out an idea, and he would highlight all the barriers, helping to eliminate them with competency. In the end, a concept would evolve into a plan that became a reality, and it would run smoothly and successfully. Everything he did had a process so it could be improved.

Efficient people are recognized for their skills and abilities. They are valued in life for what they can accomplish. They are the top five percent of the twenty percent who do eighty percent of the work in the world. Efficiency is both a gift and something that can be developed. Find an efficient person you can learn from and start taking notes. All of us are to embrace order in our lives. Without order, chaos reigns. God never intended us to live disrupted lives. He wants you to be settled, so he put within you both the skill and the ability to order it. Ask him to help you. He will.

Father, thank you for the order you created in life. I pray that it helps me to do what you want me to do efficiently.

FLEXIBLE

*When I am with those who are weak, I share their weakness, for I want to bring
the weak to Christ. Yes, I try to find common ground with everyone,
doing everything I can to save some.*

1 CORINTHIANS 9:22 NLT

Contortionists do things that we think are not humanly possible. They
bend their bodies and fit into objects that make most of us cringe. How
do they do it? Can anyone learn the art? Contortionists have a genetic
anomaly when it comes to flexibility. They then develop this into a talent
through learning and practice. All people can learn certain moves that
are beneficial in preventing injury and improving life, but not all can be
contortionists.

Our mental flexibility is also important. Throughout our lives, the
flexibility of our brain, called neuroplasticity, benefits greatly by learning
new things. God wants us to be flexible so that meeting people where
they are is not troubling, and we can find common ground with them.
God wants to show you new things and for you to practice good habits.
He asks for us to dedicate time each day to him, so we learn from him
and then share him with others.

*Jesus, help me to be flexible and not to ignore those I think are different
than me. Show me how to love all people.*

GROW AND ADAPT

When God's people are in need, be ready to help them.
Always be eager to practice hospitality.
ROMANS 12:13 NLT

One of our securities in life is to settle into a home and create a comfortable space that is safe from danger and protected from the elements. We need this as humans at a basic level in order to begin to explore deeper relationships and to develop within a community. But in this process of finding security, we face the possibility of withdrawing into ourselves and becoming self-focused. Additionally, our school or work roles may become routine and predictable. How are we challenged to grow and adapt?

Of course, God has the answer, and it is found in a unique way. Inviting strangers into our homes makes us both vulnerable and opportunistic. The good news of Christ's redemption can then be shared, and we are allowed the occasion to adapt to a new element in our lives. If you are open to meeting new people, if you can listen well, and if you desire to share your life, you can be mutually enriched by hosting people in your home. Enrichment is the beauty of being adaptable.

I want my life to be enriched by others. I don't want to isolate myself. Help me to help the person my friends don't care about, Jesus.

ADMIRATION

It is the LORD your God you must follow, and him you must revere.
Keep his commands and obey him; serve him and hold fast to him.
DEUTERONOMY 13:4 NIV

Because he was a young surfer, there were many ahead of him who rode the waves well. His respect for them was evident in how he talked of their abilities. At contests he would look for the heats where they were competing. He aimed to end up at the front of the crowd, moving between people to get closest to the shore, always driven to see a favorite surfer tearing it up. His admiration for the great surfers cast aside any temporary distraction. When he got in the water, he practiced their moves, taking from his memory, and planning out the wave, section by section. He would copy them so that eventually he would be like them, a renowned surfer who everyone knew.

Jesus is more famous than a great surfer, or artist, or sportsman. He holds the highest position in humanity being seated next to God the Father. As his follower, the more you admire him, the closer you will follow him.

Father, help me to admire you and to imagine myself doing the things Jesus did. I want you to lead me as you led Jesus. Help me to hear you today and to be obedient to your voice.

INSIGHTFUL

Bear one another's burdens,
and thereby fulfill the law of Christ.
GALATIANS 6:2 NASB

Males have a difficult time asking for help. It is a known fault. We want to figure something out on our own, and if we really get stuck, then we ask for help, maybe. Sometimes we are stubborn enough to sit in a problem for so long that it costs us our relationships. Ironically in these cases, it is often our relationships that also save us. When we can take our problems to another person and share them, it is amazing what a different perspective it can provide.

Wisdom comes to those who seek it. It's like digging for a well; you dig until water bubbles up. But you have to start digging and stick with it in order to get to the water. Understanding comes from being able to share. When you share your burdens and ask for help you can get solutions to things because your friends and family see it from a different view. Reach out to get help and help others.

God, I know I need help. Give me boldness to share with my friends and family and the wisdom to help them.

GOD'S VALUE

You created my inmost being;
you knit me together in my mother's womb.
PSALM 139:13 NIV

How much are you willing to pay for that rare item? It is incredible to read about the amount of money some people will spend on a piece of cloth from a sports hero or a rookie card. Something we would normally just throw away and replace for a few dollars can cost a bidder over four million dollars, just for something no one else has!

There is amazing scientific evidence on how each of us are uniquely created. Fingerprints, ears, eyes, tongue, and combined body movement are all ways to identify each of us individually. And, of course, our most detailed difference is our DNA. When we start to consider personality traits and spiritual gifts, we have to conclude that there are some very distinct people mingling on planet earth. Of the almost eight billion people currently on the planet right now, you are unique. That is incredible! God has made you valuable to society and to his kingdom. You cannot believe the lie that you have no worth because you are truly an exclusive item!

Jesus, show me how much you delight in me. Show me why you made me and the value I have to you.

FREEDOM

You were called to freedom, brothers.
Only do not use your freedom as an opportunity for the flesh,
but through love serve one another.
GALATIANS 5:13 ESV

Our Christian walk is one that fills us with vitality. When we see laziness creeping in, it is not a symptom of our faith; it is that we have allowed our faith to weaken. There is a strength in every believer who commits their day to God in prayer, reads his Word regularly, and has good relationships with like-minded friends. It is what helps us to remain lively.

What happens when you do not exercise, eat unhealthily, and consume volumes of high caloric drinks? Do you feel strong and full of life? No, you typically feel bloated and lazy. Watching television sounds better than playing tennis or bothering to get up and do something with others. That takes too much effort. Just bring me a pizza and something to drink. You were made to be active and to be in fellowship with other believers. That is what fills you with life and vigor. Get out and be with your friends. Seek God and do his will together.

Father, I want to be better at walking with you and seeking after you. Help me to surround myself with friends who want the same thing.

REFLECTIONS

I pray that the eyes of your heart may be enlightened in order that you may know the hope to which he has called you, the riches of his glorious inheritance in his holy people, and his incomparably great power for us who believe.
EPHESIANS 1:18-19 NIV

There is a story about two Chinese monks who were meditating. One asked the other about what they saw in each other. The older monk said he saw a stately buddha. The young monk was pleased. After a while the older monk asked the younger monk, and thinking he was sly, the younger monk replied that he saw a pile of dung. The old man smiled but did not respond. The young monk went home and proudly relayed the story to his sister. He thought he had outwitted the old monk. She laughed and mocked him, explaining that he had not outwitted anyone. What you see is what *you* are, not what *he* is.

Jesus said from inside your heart, your mouth speaks. Let your words reflect Jesus Christ and the promises you have in him!

God, help my words to reflect you and your love for other people.

SHOW CHARACTER

A man of kindness attracts favor,
while a cruel man attracts nothing but trouble.
PROVERBS 11:17 TPT

To be kind, a person must set aside their own needs and show character.
A kind man is self-aware but not seeking from others the things he
needs. Jesus, the kindest man to ever live, had everything he needed from
his Father.

As males, we desire to be strong, competent, attractive, and composed.
Jesus was all these things and more. Though he may not have been
attractive in a handsome way, he drew people to himself because of his
persona. He was dignified and secure, so people also felt assured when
they were around him. He was ready to give to others because he was not
focused on himself. You can develop kindness as a part of your character
by becoming dependent on God. Trust in him to help take care of all
your needs.

*God, I know I look to others to fulfill some of my needs. Help me to look to
you. I want to be ready to help others and not be focused on myself.*

ENDURE

Blessed is a man who perseveres under trial;
for once he has been approved, he will receive the crown of life
which the Lord has promised to those who love Him.

JAMES 1:12 NASB

His little legs pounded the trail. He was tired and his steps so small; he took twice as many as the adults around him needed to accomplish the distance. When they came across steep inclines, young men bounded up, old men gripped foliage and pulled themselves up, but he had to struggle on hands and knees, relying on his dogged determination. He said to his dad that he could do it and he wouldn't need help, so he was going to make it without asking. His mind was resolute. He would climb this mountain on his five-year-old legs. Nothing was going to stop him.

This kind of resolve shows up in all of us. What differs is the motivation and the longevity of it. In this case, there was an end goal. Some things we face do not seem to have a clear ending. We can become discouraged in the face of unclear objectives. When you are tired of fighting and feel like giving up, God comes alongside you and gives you strength.

I need your endurance, God. Give me the strength to keep walking with you.

PERFECT TRUST

When I am afraid, I put my trust in you.
In God, whose word I praise, in God I trust;
I shall not be afraid.
What can flesh do to me?

PSALM 56:3-4 ESV

It takes a lot to trust someone. They have to demonstrate that they are committed. They will sacrifice their own time and agenda for you. This builds trust. When you can really trust someone, they demonstrate that they will consistently be there for you. You can depend on them and have confidence in their responses. You know they will do what they say they will. These characteristics develop trust.

How quickly can trust go away? All it takes is one break, usually a bad one. A few little mistakes are forgivable, but a large disruption will destroy trust. There is one person, the man Jesus Christ, who will never lack commitment, sacrifice, time, consistency, or competency. He is a perfect trustworthy person, and you can know that he will not fail you. As you go about your day, be confident that Christ is with you.

I want to trust in you, God. Sometimes I get too self-reliant. I pray that you will help me to look to you more often.

SHOW FAITHFULNESS

"His master replied, 'Well done, good and faithful servant!
You have been faithful with a few things; I will put you in charge of many things.
Come and share your master's happiness!'"
MATTHEW 25:23

When we work hard at a company, we are usually rewarded with favor. It may not show up right away, but when we persevere and are hardworking, we will usually be recognized. This happens all over the world. Those who work with integrity and diligence get paid a wage that reflects this. Sometimes this hard work will even result in being promoted. You can be flipping burgers at a take-out place, or mowing lawns for a lawn care company, but when your employers see you work hard, they promote you. First it will be shift manager, then manager, then regional director, and so on. If the world works that way, and it is broken, why would a good God, whose character and decisions are perfect, not do what he says he will do by rewarding those who faithfully work for him.

Keep doing what Jesus asks of you in his Word. He doesn't ask for complex things, just that you walk as he walked. Love as he loves. He will reward you!

Jesus, I want to walk as you walked. You can help me get to my reward!

AUGUST 6

WELL DONE

"He who overcomes will inherit all this,
and I will be his God and he will be my son."
REVELATION 21:7 NIV

He had so many naysayers. People told him he couldn't do it and said
that he didn't have the right skills. It wasn't just people either. He felt like
the whole world was against him. He lacked money, training, skills, and
knowledge, yet he just knew he should do this. He had a few qualities.
He had perseverance, he had time, and he had God. So, despite what
the critics said, and regardless of his limitations, he moved forward. He
overcame the odds, and when he met Jesus after a lifetime of faithfully
serving him, he bowed before him and the King of the universe said,
"Well done, good and faithful servant."

You will face people who tell you that you are not enough. But God's
presence is in you. He gifts you with all the abilities of the Holy Spirit to
empower you to do great things. Trust in his promises to you.

*Holy Spirit, I pray that I would hear your voice. I want to set aside the
world's words and hear your wisdom.*

ADMITTING WEAKNESSES

O Lord, God of our fathers Abraham, Isaac and Israel,
keep this desire in the hearts of your people forever,
and keep their hearts loyal to you.

1 Chronicles 29:18 niv

This is a prayer we can personalize and pray all the time. As we mature, we learn that so much of our walk with God is about what he does in us rather than what we do for ourselves. This is why we ask God to keep our desires focused on him, and we pray that he will keep us loyal to him. When we try to be loyal and hungry for God, we still end up failing. In our unfaithfulness, we become saddened at our lack of strength. But when we surrender to him and rely upon him for strength, he lifts us up and enables us to walk with him.

Surrender to God. Let him know that you are not able to consistently follow Jesus the way he wants you to. When you admit your weaknesses, he will give you strength.

Jesus, I know I am young, and I want to prove myself. But I also understand that I will fail to follow you. Help me come back to you quickly. Help me surrender to you.

HANG OUT

"Listen! I am standing at the door, knocking;
if you hear my voice and open the door,
I will come into you and eat with you, and you with me."
REVELATION 3:20 NRSV

Isn't it amazing to dwell upon this thought: that the King of the universe, the owner and creator of the sun, moon, and stars, of the earth and all that is in it, asks to eat with us? Why is it that such a magnificent, powerful, and awe-inspiring being is aware of who we are? Jesus, when he was on earth, called us his friends. What an incredible picture of kindness and mercy. We are so blessed to be called the sons, friends, and family of God himself.

You may not have fully comprehended it, but when you asked Jesus to be your Savior, and you told him you would obey him, you entered into his family. Open your heart to him. Listen to his voice. He wants to hang out with you.

Jesus, I open my heart to you today. Holy Spirit, dwell with me and show me Christ. I want to hang out with you, not just know about you.

DELIVERED

Those who love me, I will deliver;
I will protect those who know my name.
When they call to me, I will answer them;
I will be with them in trouble,
I will rescue them and honor them.

PSALM 91:14-15 NRSV

He served his country in World War II at the age of nineteen. He was a chaplain and with daily diligence, he prayed Psalm 91 over himself and his men. When the enemy attacked, he saw God's protection and guidance in his decisions. After the war, he married and moved into a community of believers. There he worked every day for the rest of his life with little to no compensation except for the roof over his head and the food on his plate. He didn't complain about his life; he loved it, and he loved serving others. He died at the age of ninety-eight with Psalm 91 resonating in his ears in his final moments. He was honored by God.

When you choose to follow God and you call out to him, he will answer you. Knowing his name means you know him. Continue to seek him first and find peace in him.

Father, help me to lead my life like this man. Create in me the need to call upon you consistently and to live with gratitude regardless of my circumstances.

JOY

I prayed to the LORD, and he answered me.
He freed me from all my fears.
Those who look to him for help will be radiant with joy.

PSALM 34:4-5 NLT

Joy. It really is a happy word: short and to the point. It makes one smile when saying the word. Joy is a pleasurable feeling, but also an outward expression. It gives you the strength to dance on the grave of shame and to laugh in the face of death. That is why the Psalmist wrote that as he was freed from fear, he became radiant with joy.

The joy we receive in Christ is deep. It is much deeper than happiness, which is fleeting and likened to a stream that dries up in the heat of the summer. Joy comes from the Holy Spirit who dwells in you and gives you strength. It will rise up and sustain you like a deep spring of unending water. Be filled with joy. Smile and let that smile brighten your day.

Jesus, I want my life to be filled with joy. Take away the sadness that fills my heart at times and help me to see how your joy will give me strength.

PURIFIED

These trials will show that your faith is genuine. It is being tested as fire tests and purifies gold—though your faith is far more precious than mere gold. So when your faith remains strong through many trials, it will bring you much praise and glory and honor on the day when Jesus Christ is revealed to the whole world.

1 PETER 1:7 NLT

Gold and precious metals are still refined by fire today. There is a process to refining gold; it must be melted down by fire to be molded. Either way, purification or molding requires extreme heat. What does that look like in the believer? Must we go through tremendous trials to prove and refine our faith? For those of us not living in extreme poverty or violence of some kind (war, pestilence, or natural disaster) we have few trials really testing us. Instead, we are tested in whether or not our desire is for things other than God, such as entertainment, media, digital gadgets, etc. Do we speak as Christ would? Do we live as Christ would? Or do we look the same as those who do not follow him?

Your purity requires refinement, and that happens as you subject yourself to listening and obeying the Holy Spirit not just through external traumatic circumstances but through the daily decisions of obedience. Continue to choose to pick up your cross and follow Christ.

Jesus, I want to follow you. Help me to live as you would live and to be different than the world.

TRUE PEACE

That's where he restores and revives my life.
He opens before me the right path
and leads me along in his footsteps of righteousness
so that I can bring honor to his name.

PSALM 23:3 TPT

What is it that restores a soul? How do we find peace in a world of trauma? Our safe space is in Christ. We cannot find it in men or in their institutions. We must turn to Christ if we want to know what it means to walk on the right path and to know his goodness. Jesus, the one who made us and knows us best, is always looking out for us. He will not allow us to be destroyed. He promises to stand with us through the toughest of times and to celebrate with us in the best moments. He is our only place of true peace and restoration.

When you are troubled, and when you are overwhelmed, turn to God. The Holy Spirit is with you to bring you comfort and peace. He will restore your soul and help you know the presence of Christ.

Holy Spirit, comfort me in my trouble and make your presence known to me, so I can bring honor to Jesus' name.

INNOCENT

"I am sending you out like sheep among wolves.
Therefore, be as shrewd as snakes and as innocent as doves."
MATTHEW 10:16 NIV

Four animals are highlighted in today's verse. It is clear that wolves eat sheep, and we are to be the faithful sheep amongst the worldly wolves. So, is Jesus saying that we are going to get eaten? Yes, in many ways, we may be devoured and swallowed up by all that the world has to offer. We can become consumers who are, in the end, consumed. This is a reality of every believer.

Jesus tells us how to survive these pitfalls in life. Be as shrewd and savvy as a snake, yet innocent as gentle doves. The imagery here is powerful. We likely picture these animals as we read. Jesus wants us to be smart, but not in an evil way. He wants us to pay attention, be wise, and be ready to fly when needed. You need the Holy Spirit to give you wisdom and to show you the truth. He will assist you to live as Jesus asks in this verse.

Jesus, you both show me and instruct me on how to live. You sent your Spirit to dwell in me and to help me. Holy Spirit, please give me wisdom, truth, and strength.

GRASPING YOUR FAITH

Worship Christ as Lord of your life.
And if someone asks about your Christian hope,
always be ready to explain it.
1 PETER 3:15 NLT

When we decide to worship Jesus as the Lord of our lives, there is a change that takes place in our hearts that is undeniably obvious. When others see this change, they will ask for an explanation.

It's hard to imagine the grief of parents whose child has been taken from them, the pain of a being beaten, the violation of being stolen from, or the fear experienced in war-torn countries. How do these people forgive the perpetrators of their hardship and go on to love others ? People will ask. The simple truth is that it comes from praising Jesus and knowing him as God of all circumstances. You have been given all you need in Christ to live as a forgiving and loving person. Read and understand your Bible, hang out with other believers, and be ready to explain your faith in Christ when the time comes.

God, I know I don't fully grasp everything about you and my faith. Help me to understand more and to grow in my faith and knowledge of you.

SATISFACTION FOR THE SOUL

The fruit of the Spirit is love, joy, peace, patience, kindness, goodness,
faithfulness, gentleness, self-control; against such things there is no law.
GALATIANS 5:22-23 ESV

Do you have a favorite fruit? Do you prefer sweet and juicy or perhaps a
little tart and crunchy? There are many amazing types of fruit that God
has created. They bring us pleasure as we enjoy them. They satisfy hunger
and bring delight.

So, also, we can enjoy the fruit of the Spirit which brings satisfaction
to our souls. There is delight in doing God's will, and in particular, in
creating a place for the fruit of the Spirit to function. Imagine being self-
controlled, peaceful, joyful, and patient. What a great way to live. Think
about how those around you would also be positively impacted because
of their relationships with you. You would offer them something that is
not found in the world. This is the Spirit of Christ that dwells in you!

*Holy Spirit, fill me with your fruit and cause me to live a life that brings
delight to others.*

ONLY WAY TO GOD

Jesus said to him, "I am the way, and the truth, and the life;
no one comes to the Father except through Me."
JOHN 14:6 NASB

Many would say that there are other ways to know God apart from Jesus. However, they are wrong. Scripture makes it very clear that sin eternally separates all men from God. All men are sinners. God cannot and will not tolerate sin. He is holy. There has to be payment for our sins. The only person who has paid for the sins of all men is Jesus Christ. Therefore, he is the only one who can make a way for us to know God. No one else has this ability or right. Anyone who thinks that they know another way to God or speaks of anything other than the plan of salvation laid out by the Creator will be struck down. If they really know and see God for who he is, they would never dare.

As a follower of Christ and as one who has received his forgiveness, you need not fear. You are loved, forgiven, and cherished. You are walking in the way of truth and life. Keep following Christ.

Thank you for your forgiveness, Jesus. Help me to share your truth with others.

NEEDS OF OTHERS

The Lord God said, "It is not good for the man to be alone.
I will make a helper who is just right for him."
GENESIS 2:18 NLT

The boy ran across the grass, water spilling a little as he carefully cradled the large cup. His dad was thirsty from digging the fence posts, and he knew this would help. It was one of those beautiful days to take on an outside project, but the ground was much harder than the father had realized. Eventually, he disposed of the shovels and rented an auger. The son become even more beneficial as he was able to help his father by clearing the loose dirt after the auger had finished. As the sun set, father and son sat, satisfied that they had completed the posts and were ready for the next day.

No matter who takes what role, even if it is just to serve water, helpfulness is demonstrated in cooperating to complete a project. When you look to serve another person, you are helpful to them. This is what God calls you to do as a part of his body of believers.

God, I want to be helpful to people. I know that is what you desire for me. Show me the needs of others so I can help them.

LIVING FOR OTHERS

Everything created by God is good,
and nothing is to be rejected if it is received with gratitude.
1 TIMOTHY 4:4 NASB

What are you going to receive from the generation before you? Have you ever considered what you may inherit? Perhaps it is very little, or it may be a great deal. We may think of inheritance as what we will receive upon the death of someone in the previous generation, but it is also active now. We are receiving their traits, habits, and wisdom. Have you ever thought about it? What you have been given by the generation before you?

You have already been granted so much that you may sometimes fail to recognize traits and habits in yourself. How can you be wise about what you do with them? You must rely on the Spirit of God to develop you into the man he wants you to be. Do good with what you have been given.

God, thank you for all that you have given me. Show me what I have that you can use for your purposes and help me to not live my life for myself alone.

NOT BORING

"Call to me and I will answer you and tell you
great and unsearchable things you do not know."
JEREMIAH 33:3 NIV

Do you think of God as boring? Some people do. It is not because he is;
it is because they do not know him. But for those who know him, he is
anything but boring. He is incredible. Stop for a minute and think about
the world around you. All that you see before you, even manmade things,
are made based upon his creativity in us. Look at nature and recognize
how detailed and creative it is. Look at what your body can do, how your
brain thinks, and be amazed.

All that we see is limited by us, not by him. We are limited by our
physical eyes. When we are resurrected, we will be able to see both
natural and spiritual things. Our eyes will be opened to the incredible
splendor of God's eternity. God is excited to show you more of himself
even now.

*God, I want to see more of the great things I cannot see with my eyes. Open
my heart and mind to all that you have to show me.*

REWARDED FOR DILIGENCE

The plans of the diligent lead surely to abundance,
but everyone who is hasty comes only to want.
PROVERBS 21:5 NRSV

Diligence is rewarded. Persistence breaks down barriers. Pillars of rock in a cave are created by persistently dripping water which leave mineral deposits that form into stalactites and stalagmites. Nature demonstrates that over time, despite strong resistance, stubborn determination wins. Consistency of action that is tireless and unrelenting yields results. Perhaps there are small adjustments that need to be made when facing a difficulty, but ultimately if we are steadfast in our pattern of behavior, our effort will be rewarded.

Despite a great deal of resistance, overwhelming hatred, and incredible suffering, Christ was determined to complete his mission. He died willingly and with great difficulty for our sakes. He gives you the same strength to do the will of God.

Jesus, I want to work hard and not stop doing your will. Please strengthen me.

ACCEPTANCE

"The Father gives me the people who are mine.
Every one of them will come to me, and I will always accept them."
JOHN 6:37 NCV

Jesus' acceptance of a person seeking him is based on one criterion: faith. In our world, acceptance is more like tolerance. We put up with beliefs and behaviors that we don't agree with in order to gain the acceptance of people around us. But Jesus makes it clear he will accept all who come to him, repent of their sins, and accept him as their Lord and Savior. The difference between our tolerant world and our accepting of Christ is that no one asks Jesus into their life without a struggle. To be received by him, there is a cost.

When we look inside ourselves and recognize our brokenness and shame, we come to understand our sin. This is especially true as it relates to a holy God. His acceptance of us is complete because in order to come to him, we had to accept our true sinful natures and our need for a Savior. Jesus doesn't accept you based on how you are doing in the moment, your previous actions, thoughts, or physical state. He accepts you based on your humble belief and faith in him. He accepts you because of who he is not who you are.

Jesus, I believe in you. I thank you for your forgiveness and compassion. I need you.

REGARDED

"Notice how the lilies of the field grow; they do not labor nor do they spin thread for cloth, yet I say to you that not even Solomon in all his glory clothed himself like one of these. But if God so clothes the grass of the field, which is alive today and tomorrow is thrown into the furnace, will He not much more clothe you?"

MATTHEW 6:28-30 NASB

"Consider nature," says Jesus. Look at what occurs around you and see God in it. How does he take care of the sparrow and the flower? God is active in our lives far beyond what we realize. Yes, we are really that important to him. Even down to the colorful hairs on our heads.

Would the Father send the Son to die for that which he did not believe valuable? He would not. He could easily have left us to our own destruction. God views you as his own. He created you and came to you. He cares about you.

God, thank you for your care of me. Help me to trust you. In my trust of you, help me to learn to care for those around me.

TYPE OF WORK

People were bringing little children to Jesus for him to place his hands on them, but the disciples rebuked them. When Jesus saw this, he was indignant. He said to them, "Let the little children come to me, and do not hinder them, for the kingdom of God belongs to such as these."

MARK 10:13-14 NIV

Fostering children takes an enormous amount of work. Time is the first sacrifice. Foster parents take numerous classes and learn how to care for and support hurting children. Those hours could be spent getting other things done or enjoying life. The next thing given up is finances; adding children to a family requires buying new things for the home, new clothes for the children, and setting up dedicated space. But the real sacrifice is the disruption of the foster family's daily lives and emotional stability with the addition of brokenhearted children. This is the type of work that Jesus loves.

If your family has helped children like this, you are doing the work of Jesus. You may know others who foster children. Pray for them, and if you can, find some way to help them. It pleases the heart of God greatly.

Jesus, I pray that you would use me to help children get to know you and that I would love them like you do.

SAFETY

The Lord sees all we do;
he watches over his friends day and night.
His godly ones receive the answers they seek
whenever they cry out to him.

PSALM 34:15 TPT

Our wellbeing is wrapped up in God more than we may realize. We are a part of his family, and he enjoys being involved in our daily lives. He is not an aloof father but is very present with us in our day-to-day activities. His invitation to us is to welcome him and to recognize the personal nature of his relationship with us. He sees all we do as he watches over us.

Danger lurks everywhere, especially for those who are more vulnerable. To God, we are the vulnerable ones. He sees our troubles better than we do, and he wants to provide a place of safety for us to rest in him. He is all about building a closer relationship with each one of us. God wants you to know that he watches over you. You are safe with him.

Thank you for your care of me, God. I pray for those children who do not know you. Keep them safe and help them to know you.

REPUTABLE

Never let loyalty and kindness leave you!
Write them deep within your heart.
Then you will find favor with both God and people,
and you will earn a good reputation.
PROVERBS 3:3-4 NLT

He's the athlete. He's the class clown. He's the one who swears. He's
the Christian. We can have reputations for various things. People can
be known for excellence, trustworthiness, humor, or strategy. Some
consistently demonstrate negative traits like greed, anger, impatience, or
arrogance such that they end up with a bad reputation. Being reputable
is about being highly regarded among others who see you as sound in
thought, honest in word, and dependable in deed.

When you think of your friends or close acquaintances who have good
reputations, what characterizes them? Like Jesus, those you relate to
likely have some of the good characteristics that you appreciate. Perhaps
you are drawn to things you see in yourself that you value. The Bible talks
about bad morals corrupting the good, but the opposite is also true: those
with good morals encourage respectable behavior in those who may not
have good reputations.

*Father, I want to have a good reputation. I want to love others well and be
like you so that I am known as one who is like God.*

STUNNING

In your glory and grandeur go forth in victory!
Through your faithfulness and meekness
the cause of truth and justice will stand.
Awe-inspiring miracles are accomplished by your power,
leaving everyone dazed and astonished!

PSALM 45:4 TPT

When was the last time you were stunned, shocked into a pause? Perhaps you can recall when time stood still; your mouth may have been open, the sound changed in your ears, and your eyes were wide with wonder. It could have been from some news you received, or watching a sporting event, or seeing someone who was attractive. You may have been stunned by a painful experience like a punch, or a joyous occasion such as when you won something.

There are many moments in life when we experience being stunned; the good ones can come from surprises or exploration. Getting out and doing something new can evoke spectacular moments. It is important to integrate creativity and adventure into your routines. You were made to be more than a robot experiencing safe habits. God is a God of exploration and creativity.

I want to be stunned as I find out more about you, God. Show me who you are!

INTO YOUR FEELINGS

"Peace I leave with you, My peace I give to you; not as the world gives do I give
to you. Let not your heart be troubled, neither let it be afraid."

JOHN 14:27 NKJV

Take a moment to think of one of your favorite places as you've been
growing up. Why is it a favorite? What do you feel when you recall
it? Most often within that place, there is a sense of peace. It conjures
up feelings of rest, relaxation, and fun. When you think of that place,
can you take time to imagine God visiting you there? Perhaps see him
walking toward you across the field, the sand, or the deck. He is smiling
and pleased to see you. In your heart, there is a sense of inexpressible joy
and pleasure.

When you are stressed and anxious, when the world seems to be crashing
in on you, perhaps even when you are recalling some trauma in the past,
you need a place of peace to go to. Take time to invite God into those
feelings and allow his calm to embrace you. He can still your fears and
anxieties.

*God, I invite you into my heart to bring me peace. I don't want to be afraid
or troubled because of what I have experienced. I want to be settled because
you are my God.*

PERSUASIVE

I myself am convinced, my brothers and sisters, that you yourselves are full of
goodness, filled with knowledge and competent to instruct one another.

ROMANS 15:14 NIV

There are those people who are strongly convincing. They ooze
confidence and speak clearly about what they think. They can talk
about multiple topics with thoughtful and strong opinions. There are
also those who are persuasive because of their personalities. They have
a winning influence that is charming and warm. They make others feel
good, not just by words but because of their appeal. Then there are those
with specific deep knowledge that is well researched. They convince us
because they know what they speak about. They are the researchers and
teachers of the world.

For what purpose are you to be persuasive? To share Christ with others.
You are to be knowledgeable about who he is, to be warm like he was,
and to teach others as he did. He wants you to demonstrate his love, his
mercy, and his kindness.

Jesus, help me to be convincing when it comes to sharing who you are.
I want people to see my genuine love for you and to then be changed.

HUMOR

We laughed and laughed and overflowed with gladness.
We were left shouting for joy and singing your praise.
PSALM 126:2 TPT

Who doesn't love a good joke? When you are in the right mood, it's fun to sit down and watch a movie full of funny scenes and hilarious lines or to hang out with your friends and just laugh. There is something therapeutic about it. At times it can be easy to take things too far, and suddenly you are making jokes that you shouldn't be making. In the right group, it is simple to steer things back on track because the Holy Spirit brings a sense of purity and cleanliness. We don't need to "go there" in order to have fun.

Have you ever wondered if God is able to have fun? Why do you think he made laughter? Not because he cannot laugh! In fact, look at his creation. Perhaps he made some things simply so you can laugh. Have you ever seen a gobi jerboa or a proboscis monkey? Look them up and see what you think. There are so many different, funny things that he created. God has a sense of humor for sure.

I want to be able to laugh and have fun with you, God. Show me how to enjoy what you have made and laugh with you.

LISTENING FOR THE PLAN

When you turn to the right or when you turn to the left,
your ears shall hear a word behind you, saying,
"This is the way; walk in it."
ISAIAH 30:21 NRSV

Some of us wonder what we will do with our lives. We may look at our siblings or friends and they seem to have it all together. It's like they know just what they want to do for their education and their careers. We may know what we want to do, and the path we have laid out before us seems clear. In both circumstances, it is good to trust in the voice of God to guide us. He is with us, and if we stop to listen, he will guide us throughout our lives. He is faithful that way.

God has a plan for your life. He has created good things in you, and he has a plan for how he wants to use them. Surrender all your plans to him. Find out how to enjoy him, and he will put his desires in your heart.

God, I trust in your leadership. Help me to hear your voice and to follow your leading.

AWARE

Turn my eyes from looking at worthless things;
and give me life in your ways.
PSALM 119:37 ESV

He was young, still learning so much in life. When his parents told him he could not watch certain types of movies, he wanted to punch a wall. He was mad that they would interfere. *Why do they care, and how can silly movies hurt me anyway?* He was not aware of how much they affected him. As he grew older, he started to become mindful of himself. What was fake in movies had become reality in his mind. It affected his mood and his spirit. He was conscious of the need to guard his eyes and to keep his mind sharp for God's purposes. As he continued in this way, his prayers grew more effective. His awareness increased, and he became a mighty warrior in prayer, tearing down strongholds and breaking through spiritual darkness.

As you gain understanding of the world around you, especially in the spiritual realm, you will become more aware of what you are allowing into your heart through movies and other forms of entertainment.

Help me to protect my eyes and guard my heart, God. I know that this life offers some fun and exciting things to look at, but I want my heart to choose you.

POTENTIAL

His divine power has given us everything we need for a godly life through our
knowledge of him who called us by his own glory and goodness.

2 PETER 1:3 NIV

We all have potential within us from birth until death. We are made
uniquely with skills and gifts that are to be used for God's purposes. Yet,
we are limited by the difficulties we face in our lives, and we are beset
with personal sin. Part of our journey is to reach the potential that God
has placed in us while overcoming trouble and iniquity. It is through this
process that we build endurance and character which help uncover our
true potential. We miss potential when we try to avoid trouble and end
up becoming lazy in our faith, just avoiding difficulties.

You must turn away from sin. That isn't even a question. Apathy is the
worst enemy of your potential. As you have learned in science class at
school, potential is stored, and action, movement, and initiation are
required to unleash that potential. Keep your faith moving by being
challenged through friends, prayer, and your study of God's Word.

*God, help me not to run from difficulty. You will help me when I face the
trials that you have prepared me to walk through. I want to know your
divine power working through me.*

HE CARES

Then Jesus said, "Come to me, all of you who are weary and carry heavy
burdens, and I will give you rest."

MATTHEW 11:28 NLT

Jesus takes care of those in need. He knows what each person needs
before they even ask. It is in his nature to love and to give. The prideful
and self-sufficient won't get help from him because they have no need
of him. It is not that he rejects them; they reject him. The person who
recognizes his own failures and shortcomings and calls out to Jesus will
be answered. They will never be left alone or in need.

We all have brokenness, shame, and hurt. And none of us are perfect. We
all sin. When you agree with this and turn to Jesus, he will be there for
you. He will care for you and give you strength.

*Jesus, I know I am imperfect. I know that my failures are laid out before
you. You see everything. I thank you that despite my brokenness, you love,
care, and strengthen me.*

SEEK HIM

I know that You can do all things,
And that no plan is impossible for You.
JOB 42:2 NASB

As we learn more about God, and we start to know him personally, we understand his amazing character. It is excellent and praiseworthy. He is faithful, truthful, gentle, loving, just, and strong. When he says he will do something, he will. There is no doubting what he says. He is not flippant with his words. Jesus demonstrated this when he walked the earth. He was so close to the Father that he knew what his Father wanted. When Jesus asked for things to be done, they were done! People were healed, waters were stilled, storms ceased, and lives were transformed.

You are connected to the God of the impossible. Draw close to him and his desires will become yours. You can do the impossible. Chase after God with all your heart and show the world what a follower of Christ looks like!

Jesus, you showed me how to follow you and walk with power and authority on the earth. I need your help to seek the will of God. Change my heart to be motivated to seek you before any other thing.

CONTENT AND THANKFUL

Let your reasonableness be known to everyone. The Lord is at hand; do not
be anxious about anything, but in everything by prayer and supplication with
thanksgiving let your requests be made known to God.

PHILIPPIANS 4:5-6 ESV

What is the key to a happy life, and if we find it, will we be thankful?
Surely if we were happy our hearts would flow with thankfulness? Since
the time of Democritus (the Laughing Philosopher, Greece, 460-370
BC) and likely before, people have been searching for the definition of
happiness. His early philosophy was that happiness was found in the
soul, not in possessions. Later philosophers believed that it was found
in the balance of pleasure and pain; if there is more pleasure than pain,
then there is happiness. Christians believe that happiness is found in
contentment in Christ. When we find contentment, our hearts are in a
state of thankfulness. This is why Paul writes that in all things we should
be thankful; it is also why he was content.

Consider what it means to be thankful and be mindful of the need to
remain in a place of contentment and satisfaction with what you have.
Give thanks to God for everything he has blessed you with.

*God, I want to be content with what I have so that I can be grateful. Take
away my desire for other things and help me to be happy.*

REWARD OF RESURRECTION

Let us not grow weary of doing good,
for in due season we will reap,
if we do not give up.
GALATIANS 6:9 ESV

Receiving a reward is often related to having done something: accomplishing a task, completing a project, or winning an event. How often do we receive rewards for doing nothing? There may be a few times. A good father might call a child over once in a while and give them something they love, simply saying, "This is just for being you." This special gift requires no achievement, no task completed, and no competition won.

The Bible makes it clear that we are each going to be rewarded for our deeds on earth. For those who believe, they are rewarded for their righteousness. But it is only through faith in Christ as the substitute sacrifice that they will be rewarded. Wow, what grace and favor we receive when we clearly do not deserve it! No task needs to be accomplished, no completed project is required, and no event is to be won. All you need is faith.

Thank you, God, for rewarding me with resurrection when all I did was believe! I look forward to the day when I meet you!

UNQUESTIONABLE

May God give you more and more grace and peace as you grow in your knowledge of God and Jesus our Lord.

2 PETER 1:2 NLT

When we question life and ask the meaning of things, we usually end up at God's doorstep. We then have to wrestle with his existence, his ability, and whether or not he is controlling all of the chaos around us. We should ask questions. Any Christian worth his salt asks and wonders. When people tell you not to question, that is when you have to be cautious. God can handle our questions. Man is the one who worries about how they will be answered. God is okay with our doubts too. He wants us to come to him with our concerns and not hide them. Look at how he handled his disciple Thomas. He made himself real in the way that Thomas asked him to. Jesus told Thomas to put his fingers into the wounds in his sides where the stakes had nailed him to the cross just days before in order to alleviate Thomas' doubts. God has strong character.

When you realize he does not deviate from who he is, the answers often come. You can trust in God to give you peace and answer all your questions.

Lord, you have all the answers and I have a ton of questions. Help me to trust in your character and never stop asking you questions.

AGAINST THE ODDS

Though we walk in the flesh, we are not waging war according to the flesh.
For the weapons of our warfare are not of the flesh but have divine power
to destroy strongholds.

2 CORINTHIANS 10:3-4 ESV

Can you imagine entering a war where your enemy has guns and all you have are basic weapons like clubs and knives? There are very few wars that have been waged like this except early in history when westerners faced natives in foreign lands. Who would knowingly enter a battle with such overwhelmingly poor odds?

God is not unaware of this in your life either, not that you wage physical wars, but you do have spiritual battles. Perhaps you are not aware of them. God has equipped you with everything you need to do battle with the enemy. You also have a body of believers that you can rely on in times of struggle because each person has been equipped with different gifts. Your weaknesses are covered by the strengths of others. Pray with your friends and talk about spiritual matters with them.

Thank you for my friends who believe in you, God. Help us to be aware of the battles going on around us and to pray together more often.

SYMPATHETIC

All of you, be like-minded, be sympathetic,
love one another, be compassionate and humble.
1 PETER 3:8 NIV

Jesus sympathizes with us in our weaknesses. He was concerned for us from long ago. He didn't stand back but fully threw himself headlong into our mess. His compassion and kindness were demonstrated in his sacrifice, and that is important to note. Sympathy does not occur without being willing to take the focus off yourself and allow time for the consideration of what others are experiencing. When we have thought about others, we can act with kindness, love, and humility. And that humility means that we place others before ourselves.

Jesus could have stayed with his Father. He chose to come for you and to experience what you do. He faced your fears, temptations, anxieties, and feelings. He felt your joy, laughter, and pleasure. He knew what it was to be human. As fully God and man, he prays for you with true sympathy.

Jesus, I want to know you more so I can be helped by you. You know how to live this life and to do it well so please show me your ways.

PERFECTION

The word of the LORD is right and true;
he is faithful in all he does.
PSALM 33:4 NIV

Think of a person who has never lied. There are people who turn up when they say they will. There are people who do not waste words; when they speak, all others are quiet because what they say is profound and true. But does a perfect person exist on earth? No. There may, however, be some men who have devoted themselves to listening so that they do not speak unwisely. Some men who, as James writes, have a measure of ability to hold their tongues. But there are none, now or ever in the past, except Jesus Christ, who has always spoken perfectly. His Word is true, and his ways are excellent. There is no one like him.

You serve a perfect God who speaks truth and is faithful in all that he does. Allow this word to seep into your heart and give you confidence today as you go out into the world. The greatest being in the universe is on your side!

Jesus, thank you for being on my side. I pray that it helps me to love others better and to show the same care that you did. I ask for your strength.

GREATNESS

The LORD set his affection on your ancestors and loved them,
and he chose you, their descendants, above all the nations—as it is today.
DEUTERONOMY 10:15 NIV

It can be overwhelming for a father to raise a mini-me. Sometimes it is easier with daughters because he may feel less pressure raising a different gender. After all, he can just blame the mother. Ha! But for a dad, having a son is an amazing experience. So much of him will be reflected in the son. Perhaps this is the worry that dads feel because they have trouble loving themselves. Your dad may have thought about this too. He may struggle with things in himself that he sees in you.

When you come to realize that a good Father, God, created you, and you accept that he affectionately loves you, you can be both a better son, and in the future, a better father. Your confidence can come from the fact that God chose you and he calls you his son.

God, you are great, and you chose me! Help me to place my confidence in you because of how great you are.

NEVER ABANDONED

The Sovereign LORD is my strength!
He makes me as surefooted as a deer,
able to tread upon the heights.
HABAKKUK 3:19 NLT

Hiking a mountain is an exhilarating experience even if you are not scaling rock faces. The effort put into a trek is rewarded in short breaks with beautiful views. Then there are the uncertain times, when the footing is treacherous, or cliffsides are too steep to simply walk up. Guide ropes may be present to help you walk around the danger and to keep your balance, but often before you take a hold, you test them. You wisely pull on the rope to make sure it seems firm. *Can I trust this to keep me safe?*

God gives you his assurance that you can always rely on him. He will not allow you to slip and fall. His promise is to keep you firmly in his grasp and to never let you go. Jesus relied on this security even when those around him abandoned him. His friends and family failed him, but he never faltered because God made his steps sure.

God, you are my strength. Continue to help me trust in you. Show me where I am self-reliant, and gently bring me back to security in you.

INCREDIBLE

The LORD merely spoke,
and the heavens were created.
He breathed the word,
and all the stars were born.
PSALM 33:6 NLT

Stop for a minute and listen to the sounds around you. Have you ever studied how the ear works? Consider this: sounds make vibrations in the air that are captured by the shape of our outer ear and the inner canal. These sound waves cause the eardrum to vibrate which sets three miniscule bones into motion. This movement stirs fluid into motion. That same movement bends tiny hairs in the fluid which then turn that into electrical signals. These signals are sent along our auditory nerve into our brain where we interpret sound. *Incredible.*

It is amazing to pause and take time to consider what God has made. When you do, you begin to realize how incredible he is. It causes us to speak expressions of praise and worship because he is worthy.

God, I marvel at the amazing things you do. Thank you for how incredible you are.

ABILITY

I can do everything through Christ,
who gives me strength.
PHILIPPIANS 4:13 NLT

God has given every one of us abilities. Whether great or small in our own eyes, God intends for those abilities and strengths to be used significantly for the kingdom. When we read Scriptures like the one above, or when Paul wrote about God's strength showing up when he was weak, we may feel that we cannot rely on our own abilities to accomplish things. Perhaps God is displeased that we are not relying on him more? This feeling is not of God.

He wants you to use your talents for him. In fact, he uniquely made you and gave you abilities to use for him. If you hold back, you end up only using them to promote yourself; your talents are naturally in you so they will be used without awareness or effort. You can choose to use them for God and not yourself.

God, thank you for the abilities you have given me. I pray that you would strengthen me to use them for your kingdom and not for myself. Show me how to do this.

GOOD WORK

I am sure of this, that he who began a good work in you
will bring it to completion at the day of Jesus Christ.
PHILIPPIANS 1:6 ESV

It is that last piece of the puzzle, the homework has been handed in to
the teacher, the last dish has been washed, the big jump into the pool
after the chores are finished. Ahh, it is complete. There is a good feeling
when you finish something you've worked hard on. It can be addictive.
Successful people are driven by this feeling; they love to work to
completion. If their day ends without it, they may feel dissatisfied. God
is also dissatisfied by incompletion. He will not relent until his work is
complete. His goal of dwelling with man on an earthly kingdom will be
completed. He is a finisher.

You are a part of God's work that he is finishing. He will make you into
the son that he desires, and he is patient. He works diligently on you to
prepare you for the return of Jesus.

*Thank you, God, for working on me. I ask that you would continue to
soften my heart toward you and show me what you are doing in me so we
can work together.*

RELIANCE

He has told you, mortal one, what is good;
And what does the LORD require of you
But to do justice, to love kindness,
And to walk humbly with your God?
MICAH 6:8 NASB

Mortality, death, the end of life; we all face it, and we must think about it. All we have done and will do up until we die will be accounted for. Even at our young age, we have to consider that we are facing death one day and we will face God in the end. So, how should we live considering this? He tells us first of all to love him and love others as ourselves. This verse explains what that looks like. We are to live justly, love kindness, and walk in humility. If we strive to do these things, the end will not be daunting but joyful.

Within you dwells the Spirit of Christ. As you rely on him, he enables you to live with justice, kindness, and humility. Ask him to help you walk as Jesus walked.

Holy Spirit, you are in me to help me walk as Jesus walked. Show me his ways and give me strength to rely upon you daily.

TRUE SOURCE

Jesus said to her, "I am the resurrection and the life. Whoever believes in me, though he die, yet shall he live, and everyone who lives and believes in me shall never die. Do you believe this?"

JOHN 11:25-26 ESV

When you think of the word *powerful,* what comes to mind? Maybe to you it means the blast of a rocket as it leaves the earth? Or possibly you think about the power behind a natural disaster? Some people are extremely powerful, like a mixed martial arts fighter. Some people are not physically strong, but their persuasive powers can influence thousands.

God for sure comes to mind. He is the source behind power because he created the potential for natural disasters, the fuel for rockets, the muscles, the mind, and voices of men. Love is his nature, and that love did the most powerful thing we know yet—it overcame death. No one escapes death. It is the most powerful negative force we know. Of all the others named above, death tends to be the most feared. We often fear it because it seems so final and unknown. But Jesus overcame that most powerful enemy. Now we have life, and we have the power of the resurrected Savior in us. Nothing can take that away from us.

Jesus, you are powerful! I pray that you would remind me of your power in me. Show me how to live so others would learn about you and believe in you.

DYNAMIC

Never doubt God's mighty power to work in you and accomplish all this. He
will achieve infinitely more than your greatest request, your most unbelievable
dream, and exceed your wildest imagination! He will outdo them all, for his
miraculous power constantly energizes you.

EPHESIANS 3:20 TPT

God is incredible. His purpose in creation is underlined by his love and
his justice. Because of his love, we receive mercy, and because of his
justice, this evil world will be made right. We can be confident that if we
ask according to his will, he will do what he wants to accomplish in us.
There is no limit to what he can do. Think of what he has made; consider
the universe, this planet, and all its inhabitants. The intricate details
demonstrate his dynamic power.

You can ask God to show you what he wants to do, and when he does,
ask him to move through you in power. He will accomplish amazing
things through you when you talk to your Father.

*Jesus, like you, I want to hear from the Father and do his will. Show me
how to listen and walk closely with him as you did. I want to be an example
of the dynamic power of God.*

STRONG FAITH

Faith is confidence in what we hope for
and assurance about what we do not see.
HEBREWS 11:1 NIV

As we grow up, we dream of making something of ourselves. When we were little, we would think about being a doctor, or a soldier, or a policeman, or a fireman. We wanted to fill the role of a hero. Did we have a strong confidence about being one of those people? Would we take any steps to learn to be like them? Not likely. The thought that we were going to do any of these jobs as a career was not based on anything more than a temporary childish desire. Assurance of our faith, however, is not based on a fleeting passion; rather, on the confidence and conviction that Jesus is who he says he is. Jesus offers this security because he demonstrated it in his role as the only true hero paying the ultimate cost to save all people from their sins.

You are one of the reasons that Jesus did what he did. He wants you in his kingdom. Be confident today that he is with you and has things for you to do.

Father, strengthen my faith and help me to be sure of what you have done and will do in my life.

NEEDS NOT YOUR OWN

*My children, we should love people not only with words and talk,
but by our actions and true caring.*
1 JOHN 3:18 NCV

If you were to enter the hospital as a patient today, what sort of caretaker would you want? If you were at home and unable to take care of yourself, who would you want by your side? According to research, people want care that comforts, confirms, and builds relationships. People want friends with them when they are suffering. They also want to know that they matter and that they are important. A lot of people want their mothers when they are hurting.

When we consider attributes of mothers and friends, hopefully these words come to mind: kind, thoughtful, considerate, loving, gentle, sensitive, and attentive. This defines a caring person. Christ was a caring gentleman. He loved those around him and helped those in need. He healed many and grieved with those who grieved. He was an example of a truly caring friend. Demonstrate Christ to your friends and family by showing them that you care about them and are considerate of their needs.

Jesus, you were great at loving people, and I want to be like that. Give me your strength today as I try to love and care for my friends and family.

THE BEST STANDARDS

Confess your sins to each other and pray for each other
so that you may be healed.

JAMES 5:16 NIV

As young men, we feel a social responsibility to be strong, unfailing, and brave. This is not a task that we accept willingly. There is an internal sense that we must be this way. So, when it comes to confessing our weaknesses to our friends, we have a very difficult time. It creates trouble in our hearts. We want to be strong and prove ourselves, but confessing our sins leaves us feeling weak and broken. Feeling this way makes it hard to speak about any area of failure, whether at school, work, or home, or even within ourselves.

You may have high standards for the way you want to live. Ultimately, nothing is higher than Jesus' standard. He is and should be your measurement in all realms. What is amazing, and also a great relief, is his grace for you and your multiple failures. He is the standard and the final accounting. He has mercy on you, and his grace empowers you to choose to live for him.

Thank you, Jesus, for your mercy toward me.

GOD AUTHORS CONFIDENCE

We are confident of all this because of our
great trust in God through Christ.

2 CORINTHIANS 3:4 NLT

People who are confident are able to carry more burdens in life. Why? Because those burdens tend to weigh less. Those who are confident don't carry a lot of doubts. They believe in what they are doing, they know they can do it, and their focus is given to improving situations, problem solving, and working hard. Doubts trouble the mind and inhibit effectiveness.

It is God's intention that his people are confident. He wants his Church to trust in him to do what is needed. Confidence and trust are tied together in this way: they work to provide security of mind and help in completing tasks. Doubt and fear attempt to break apart this God-oriented combination and these only come from one person—Satan. God is the author of confidence. Satan works to undermine that blessing. Place your confidence in God and his ability to work in you regardless of how you feel. He is with you and when you follow his leading, nothing can overcome you!

God, help me to follow you and trust in you always.

RUN TO GOD

If we confess our sins,
he is faithful and just to forgive us our sins
and to cleanse us from all unrighteousness.

1 JOHN 1:9 ESV

Jesus makes it simple for us to come to him, but we still have to do something we find difficult—humble ourselves. No man enjoys doing that. Do you like saying sorry? No. Do you enjoy it? Probably not. We are resistant to taking the blame. Yet, all we have to do is say, "Yes, God, I have sinned, and I need your mercy." When we do, he is quick to forgive, and he never denies us. He is faithful. He is also righteous because he paid for our sins. He bled and died because of them. He is the only just and righteous one to forgive us.

When you sin, do not stay away from God. Run back to him. Do so quickly and make things right. He will forgive you.

Great God who is merciful and forgiving, thank you for your mercy and kindness toward me!

ETERNITY

"Just as the Father raises the dead and gives them life,
so also the Son gives life to those he wants to."
JOHN 5:21 NCV

Have you ever wondered about eternity and living forever? How does that work? What will we do? It is a great question to ponder in our hearts. What discomfort do we have about living forever? Hopefully, none when we realize what God promises us.

Let's start in the Garden of Eden. Adam and Eve had a perfect relationship. They were not ashamed as they walked with God and amongst the animals in nature, free of guilt, fear, and pain. Their minds were not clouded with sin, nor were their eyes darkened by it. A good bet is that they could see and hear better than we ever could. They had great security in body, mind, and spirit. They were directly connected with God. They spent evenings with him! That, in a nutshell, is being truly alive. When Jesus comes back, resurrects you into eternal life, and restores creation, you will have the life described here. You will be forever alive!

God, help me to be steadfast and secure in my walk with you. I want to receive the reward of eternal life!

SHEPHERD

Even though I walk through the darkest valley,
I will fear no evil, for you are with me;
your rod and your staff, they comfort me.
PSALM 23:4 NIV

Imagine you are a sheep. You are out in the wild. What is protecting you? What skills do you have to evade predators? What wits do you have in order to overcome obstacles that come your way? When we imagine and allow ourselves time to consider a verse like this, we realize what risky lives sheep live in a world full of predators. They definitely need a smart, skilled, and equipped shepherd. One with a rod and staff is a comfort to them and he will guide them through the dangers in life to rest and refreshment in a safe place.

You live in a world full of danger. You may not even see all that is around you that God protects you from. You can be confident of his guardianship over you; he is keeping you safe. Eventually, you will make it through this life and find eternal rest and peace with him.

God, I want to have rest and peace with you in the future, but I also want it now. Help me today to trust in your protection and listen to your voice.

ACKNOWLEDGED

"Whoever acknowledges me before others,
I will also acknowledge them before my Father in heaven."
MATTHEW 10:32 NIV

It is interesting to watch an award ceremony and take notice of the back patting that occurs. A great player will stand up and say he couldn't have done it without his team or his coach. The coach will say his success was attributed to his players. How many times do we see a player stand up and say, "That was all me; I made it happen"? Not often in team sports. If someone did, they would be disliked by peers and coaches. No man is really that great on his own.

Jesus makes it clear that at the end when he comes back, he will know who accredited the blessings and gains to him and who took the glory for themselves. You may think of this verse in terms of oppression when you are beaten or harmed in an attempt to have you deny God, but you also need to think of this in the context of your daily life. How much can you say your success is really attributed to you alone?

Jesus, my life belongs to you. I admit that I am helpless to follow you on my own. I need you.

COMPETENT

The things you have heard me say in the presence of many witnesses entrust to reliable people who will also be qualified to teach others.

2 TIMOTHY 2:2 NIV

Who is competent to teach? The Bible makes it clear that there are some requirements to teach the Word. You must start by having learned from good teaching. You must be a disciple of that good teacher. And you must be reliable. But these traits alone do not qualify or demonstrate competency.

Knowledge alone does not make someone competent in the Word. They must demonstrate ability with the necessary experience and the appropriate training. When a person is skilled enough, they may be deemed competent. We have this process in many areas of learning when you engage material to learn, but you must practice to become licensed. As a disciple of Jesus, continue practicing his teaching and live as he lived. He wants you to teach others to be disciples too.

Jesus, I am not qualified on my own. I know that I have a lot to learn, but I ask that you would help me gain knowledge of you in my actions, mind, and heart.

VULNERABLE AND UNASHAMED

Make every effort to give yourself to God as the kind of person he will approve.
Be a worker who is not ashamed and who uses the true teaching in the right way.
2 TIMOTHY 2:15 NCV

The cost of being completely vulnerable with those you love and respect is huge. But that is what it takes to be unashamedly you. Unashamed people are people who care. They have deep compassion, vulnerability, and authenticity. They understand their importance in the lives of others, especially in light of Christ's purpose for them. He is their everything and they have complete trust in him.

When you fully accept yourself in Christ, life changes. No longer do you fear exposure and rejection. No longer are you driven into hiding. You are not threatened by bold emotional expressions. You are unapologetic for who you are because you are in Christ, living exactly as God intended. You can be fully yourself. You will have more compassion and care for others because you care for yourself. You have less judgment toward others because you understand what it takes to become truly authentic.

God, I want to be unashamed because I am confident in how you have made me. Help me to rely on you so I am fully equipped to be me!

MY WITNESS

When we cry, "Abba! Father!" it is that very Spirit
bearing witness with our spirit that we are children of God.
ROMANS 8:15-16 NRSV

When you sign a document that needs to be submitted formally, it requires a witness. This is common throughout legal systems across the globe. It ensures that a signature on a document is not forged, which means both the signee and the guarantor are credible.

God's promises need no witness. He says in the above verse, however, that the Spirit is a witness that we are his children. We need the Spirit of God as our witness. God is the guarantor of our resurrection, and the Spirit is the witness that ensures we are the recipients. When you come into God's kingdom, he calls you his child, and you call him "Father," or "Abba." Because you are his child, he will keep you safe and bring you into his home.

Abba, Father, thank you for making me a part of your huge family! I pray that you would keep me safe, fill me with your Spirit, and make me a witness for you.

THOUGHTFUL ENCOURAGEMENT

As we pray to our God and Father about you,
we think of your faithful work, your loving deeds,
and the enduring hope you have because of our Lord Jesus Christ.

1 THESSALONIANS 1:3 NLT

What do people say about you? Do they think of you in a positive or negative manner? Many times, we worry about what others think, which usually means they are also wondering what we think about them! What if we started sharing with people the positive things we think about them? What a great encouragement that would be. That is what Paul is writing here, to encourage the believers in Thessalonica who were faithfully working, loving each other, and continuing to hope in God. They were doing this because Jesus Christ was in them.

Because Christ is in you, choose some friends or family to encourage. Think about the positive things you see in them and communicate those things to them.

God, help me to encourage others. Show me ways I can share with them your kindness and joy.

MADE TO GIVE

Let each one give as he purposes in his heart, not grudgingly or of necessity;
for God loves a cheerful giver.
2 CORINTHIANS 9:7 NKJV

When we were children, we were so excited about Christmas. We would lay awake at night thinking about what tomorrow would bring. Then we would wake up early on Christmas morning and run out to stare at the presents under the tree. Our parents didn't necessarily buy a ton of presents, but we didn't care because we were excited about whatever we were getting. Little did we know that their joy was in watching us receive the gifts that they gave us. Much greater than getting, was the giving.

That's the secret of this verse too. There is a joy in giving that far surpasses any short pleasure that receiving gives us. You were made to give, both in your actions and with your heart. Jesus wants you to be a cheerful giver who is unrestrained in pouring yourself out for others because you do it for him.

Jesus, I want to learn to give to others so that it strengthens them. I also want to learn the joy of it for my own life.

POSSESSIONS

Jesus, looking at the man, loved him and said, "There is one more thing you need to do. Go and sell everything you have, and give the money to the poor, and you will have treasure in heaven. Then come and follow me."

MARK 10:21 NCV

When we compare ourselves to others, there is little benefit for us. Most often we either become proud of our position or unhappy with what we have. There is no middle ground. The best thing comparison can do is help us strive to improve ourselves or increase what we have. But the downside to this is that we end up living to pursue possession, status, and power.

What would it look like if we compared ourselves to Christ? What if we look to him as we strive to be like him, instead of chasing after all that the world offers? Look at what you have today and be thankful. Choose to be content with what you own so you are not like the rich man who cannot give up what he has in order to follow God.

God, thank you for all that you have given me. Help me to want what you have blessed me with and to not chase this world and what it has to offer. You have the best for me!

DELIVERANCE

He has delivered us from the domain of darkness
and transferred us to the kingdom of his beloved Son,
in whom we have redemption, the forgiveness of sins.
COLOSSIANS 1:13-14 ESV

It is likely that none of us have been trapped to the point where we have given up on life. Imagine you are out hiking and find a cool cave to explore. While you are in the cave, the entrance randomly collapses, and you are confined to darkness. No one knows where you are, and there is very little hope of being rescued. What would you feel? Likely, you would experience fear, anxiety, and hopelessness. Think of all the regrets and sadness surrounding that moment. After days of suffering emotional distress and physical pain, a stranger happens upon the cave and calls out. *Rescue! Deliverance!* What incredible joy and unbelief would overcome you.

This is what Christ has done for you, for all mankind. You no longer live in fear of death; you no longer are a slave to sin. You have been set free from these things. You have been given life and the strength to live it fully. Go out and proclaim the goodness of God who wants to redeem all of your friends.

Thank you, God! I praise you for your deliverance. I ask that you would speak through me to my friends that they too could know your salvation.

DESTINY

Let no corrupt word proceed out of your mouth,
but what is good for necessary edification,
that it may impart grace to the hearers.

EPHESIANS 4:29 NKJV

There's a saying out there that goes like this: "Watch your thoughts because they become words, and your words become actions, and your actions become habits, and habits form character, and character determines your destiny." It can be summed up in this way: "What you speak today can determine who you are in the future." Jesus said that the mouth speaks what the heart is full of. We ought to be guarding how we speak, as it does eventually mark the man we will become.

You are not a slave to your thoughts. You can determine what you say and what you don't say. Practice pausing before speaking. Practice listening with both ears before you speak with one mouth.

Jesus, I want to be someone who speaks honorably and has good character. Help me to become that man.

BELIEVE

"I will ask the Father, and he will give you another Helper, to be with you forever, even the Spirit of truth, whom the world cannot receive, because it neither sees him nor knows him. You know him, for he dwells with you and will be in you."

JOHN 14:16-17 ESV

The Bible makes it clear that deceit will be common in the final days of this world. Jesus encourages us not to be deceived but to be alert. He wants us to watch and to not be caught up in the hype of this age. We have been given a treasure to protect in the Spirit of truth. He is with us always, bringing to light the deceit of men, of ourselves, and of the Evil One.

This is how you will know when Jesus returns; his Spirit will confirm with your spirit. But you should also be careful not to be alone in this. You are to remain in the body of Christ, so you do not become deceived yourself. The Spirit of Christ operates within the context of the Church, not apart from it.

Jesus, I want to always be a person who remains a part of your church. Help me not to run away from you or from those who believe in you.

REDEMPTION

Through him to reconcile to himself all things, whether on earth or in heaven, making peace by the blood of his cross. And you, who once were alienated and hostile in mind, doing evil deeds, he has now reconciled in his body of flesh by his death, in order to present you holy and blameless and above reproach before him.

COLOSSIANS 1:20-22 ESV

Redemption is a great word. There is something satisfying about buying something back that you lost, restoring it to its rightful owner. To redeem something from wherever it is and bring it home creates satisfaction and a sense of order especially if it is something precious. Who redeems something that is not precious?

What a great act God made in redeeming us. He chose to abandon Christ to death for our sake in order to redeem us. Then Christ demonstrated his power over death by being resurrected and is now seated at the right hand of the Father, praying for us. But our restoration does not stop there, for we will be refurbished to be like him in our resurrection and we will dwell together forever! God will restore everything to its rightful place.

I praise you, God, for your great plan of redemption and how you made it happen for me. I ask that you would help me to continue to share with others how great a God you are.

RICH

Every good action and every perfect gift is from God.
These good gifts come down from the Creator of the sun, moon, and stars,
who does not change like their shifting shadows.

JAMES 1:17 NCV

We are blessed. It takes time to appreciate this. So often our minds are cluttered with reminders of what we don't have, but if we can stop and look at the things we do have, we will realize that we are very fortunate. Why can we confidently say we are blessed? The greatest reason for this is found in our security in Christ. We have assurance of a resurrection to life. Not just to any life, but a restored earth and garden of Eden kind of life. It's far beyond what we can see or imagine.

This is the blessing held in Christ. He forgave our sins and is our representative before God for every sin until we part from this world. Add to this all the blessings we have in relationships, homes, food, clothing, education, and country. Also add the goodness of God's creation and our part in history, and we start to catch a picture of the bountiful blessings that we have. You have these blessings and can recount them daily.

Jesus, I want to remember all the good things I have in you. If I forget and become overwhelmed with the world, bring me to a place where I can remember all that you have given me.

HIS BELOVED CHILDREN

When justice is done,
it is a joy to the righteous
but terror to evildoers.
PROVERBS 21:15 ESV

We want to be on the side of mercy when it comes to Judgment Day. None of us want to face a holy God who is pouring out his angry justice on those who have hurt his precious creation, or especially on those who have hurt his beloved children. We all belong to God, but some have chosen to defy him and side with Satan. On that day when God makes everything right, those of us who remain must claim our faith in Jesus Christ and his precious blood over our lives. It is the only way we can be justified. Jesus is our justification before God. There is no other way to receive the mercy of God; we are redeemed with the blood of Jesus.

As a disciple of Christ, your forgiveness of sins and your resurrection to life everlasting is contingent on your belief in Jesus. Follow him with absolute devotion; make him your one and only passion.

Jesus, I need you. I pray that my heart would be devoted to following you and obeying you alone. I want to be resurrected into life everlasting.

OCTOBER 8

PART OF THE PLAN

"Everyone who asks will receive.
The one who searches will find.
And everyone who knocks will have the door opened."

LUKE 11:10 NCV

The context of this verse is important because we know that if we go and knock on a safe full of gold it will not open. We can look for money everywhere, but we will not find it, and if we ask for a million dollars, it will not be given to us. So, what's up with that? The main context is need, not desire. God will provide for what we need, but it is based on his wisdom and not on our wants. The key is in living close to him so that we know what he wants. We learn then to desire what he desires for us.

To align your heart with God's, you must devote yourself to him. Seek friends that love God, read his Word, and spend time in prayer. Make these disciplines a part of your life and you will receive what you ask for because it will be aligned with God's will for you. You will find what you seek because the doors will be opened to you.

God, I want to devote my heart to you. I want to know what you desire, and I want to be a part of your plan to make it happen.

MEANINGFUL

Everything you speak to me is like joyous treasure,
filling my life with gladness.
PSALM 119:111 TPT

Etymology is the study of words, their meanings, and their origins.
It explains the changes over generations. Because we are becoming a
society that is technology- oriented, we have lost some of the art of
words. We are a video-first world. We have expanded what we can do on
a screen, and we've created visual masterpieces. In the process, however,
we have lost much of what we create on paper. There is no replacement
for what the mind can do when reading. We create evocative pictures in
our minds that cannot be replicated on a screen.

The saying that "a picture is worth a thousand words" is true, but we
must not count out what God designed for our beautiful minds. Reading
words creates thousands of imaginations individually tailored to each
person. When something is meaningful in whatever form it comes, it
stimulates our imagination. Christ wants your mind to be meaningfully
engaged in his Word.

*Jesus, give me a desire to read your Word and know you better through it.
Holy Spirit, help me to understand Jesus more as I read the Scriptures.*

THE BETTER CHOICE

This I pray, that your love may abound still more and more in real knowledge
and all discernment, so that you may approve the things that are excellent, in
order to be sincere and blameless until the day of Christ.

PHILIPPIANS 1:9-10 NIV

There are friends we have who seem to know every topic. Their
knowledge has a depth to it that others do not possess. You may be that
friend. It is a gift to have a mind that holds and recalls information. It is
also a delight to talk with such friends. They have a perspective that is
valuable especially when it is combined with humility.

Our knowledge, whether shallow or deep, should lead us to better
discernment in determining right from wrong. It should help us to
approve what is right and excellent and encourage the better choice. For
this to be so, you must increase your understanding of God and your
experiences in him. You should seek out his perspective and become
learned in his ways so you can imitate him and be ready for his return.

*Lord, fill me with knowledge of you, not so that I am proud, but so that I
understand you and your ways more.*

OCTOBER 11

APPROACHABLE

O God in Zion, to you even silence is praise!
You who answers prayer,
all of humanity comes before you with their requests.
PSALM 65:1-2 TPT

There is joy in knowing that there are zero restrictions to approaching God. Through Christ, he made it completely open for anyone to approach him in any state of brokenness. God has such great compassion for us. He loves his children and longs for us to come to him with our praises and our requests. He is not overwhelmed by us. No father who loves his child gives him a stone when he asks for bread. God is better than we are, and he gives good gifts.

God is not the Santa of the skies, so you want to ask for things that make sense for his kingdom, but he does want you to come and sit with him.

God, I do want to know you better. I pray that I would be patient when I come to you. Help me to not be distracted. Help me to learn discipline in my prayer life.

ONE HUNDRED PERCENT

Devote yourselves completely to the LORD our God,
walking in his statutes and keeping his commandments, as at this day.
1 KINGS 9:1 NRSV

God loves it when we pursue him fully. However, it is hard to keep that up all the time. No one is capable of doing something 100 percent of the time because it is not the way life goes. So, what does it look like to devote ourselves to God when life comes at us? We cannot all be monks, and even monks have to cook and clean to live. Our devotion to God is all about making him first in our daily choices and submitting our hearts' intentions to him. When we do this, he is honored. We can clean the bathroom and honor God! Additionally, many of our decisions end up pleasing him because we are aware of him as we live out our day.

Give yourself room to fail God and not always be the best. He is forgiving and gracious. He still wants you to give it your best, but he does not expect perfection from you.

Jesus, help me to devote myself to you and accept your grace when I fail.

RECONCILIATION

Bearing with one another and, if one has a complaint against another,
forgiving each other; as the Lord has forgiven you, so you also must forgive.
COLOSSIANS 3:13 ESV

For years he held onto the words his father had said to him. He was now a man and no longer a "skinny adolescent punk," yet he still felt the bite of each syllable. "Why does he have to be so pigheaded?" "Why can't he see things my way?" "Why can't I let this go?" He moved on in thought, troubled that he continued to think about it. He needed some peace, and it had to come by talking to his father. He had not been able to make himself seek it out since the fight. His mom had passed away, and if she were around, they may have settled the matter sooner. But they couldn't even come together at the funeral. How sad.

It is painful to hear of lives torn apart by arguments and loss. Unfortunately, it is common. God calls you to be a person of peace: to be reconciled to others and to forgive. He made a way where there was not a way, forgiving you for your sin. Because of his suffering to bring reconciliation, you can find strength to reconcile with others.

Father, help me to love well and to make peace with those who have offended me.

WHAT THE FATHER DOES

"Very truly, I tell you, the Son can do nothing on his own, but only what he sees the Father doing; for whatever the Father does, the Son does likewise. The Father loves the Son and shows him all that he himself is doing; and he will show him greater works than these, so that you will be astonished."

JOHN 5:19-20 NRSV

If we can get to a place where our lives are closely aligned with God's Word, we will find him using us to do mighty things for his kingdom. This is what Jesus is stating in today's verse from the book of John. If we do what the Father does, and he does amazing things, then amazing things will be done in our lives as well! Jesus lived his life listening to the Father through the Holy Spirit who dwelled with him. He was very attentive to the voice of God from early in his life and he spent hours in prayer and waiting on God to speak to him.

The Father wants you to have the same relationship with him that Jesus did. He has given you all that you need to pursue him in the same way.

Jesus, teach me how to walk as you did and to patiently seek you with all of my heart.

UNITY

Make my joy complete by being of the same mind,
maintaining the same love, united in spirit,
intent on one purpose.
PHILIPPIANS 2:2 NASB

Tug-of-wars are contests in which two teams struggle to capture and maintain the balance of power through pulling on a rope. If you can get your opponent's team off balance, you can overpower them. In a tug-of-war battle, team members can pull as individuals, or they can pull in unity. When unified, the strength of the individuals is magnified because the weight and force combine in one movement. It is often the breakthrough required to win a battle.

Unity within the body of believers is not that different. When we combine our wills with a united purpose, we can accomplish greater things. It is the intent of Paul to encourage us to unite for this reason. When we do, the Holy Spirit will come upon the church in greater measure. This means the world will see the power of God manifest in his people. Keep good relationships with those friends of yours who love God. Living and working in unity with each other is critical to maintaining our faith and showing the world how the love of God keeps us together.

Father, keep my friends who love you close to me. Help me to love and serve them.

FIRMLY ROOTED

Walk in Him, having been firmly rooted
and now being built up in Him and established in your faith,
just as you were instructed, and overflowing with gratitude.
COLOSSIANS 2:6-7 NASB

If we ever struggle with gratefulness, it is usually because we have lost sight of what we have. We can also become too hung up with wanting more. Paul writes that he is thankful at all times. If we ponder this and the life that he actually had, it should stir a sense of wonder in us. How could he be thankful in all things at all times? He dealt with great suffering. He was beaten, mistreated, and disparaged for the sake of Christ, yet he was thankful. How?

Paul kept his eyes on Christ and the hope that he had firmly fixed upon his resurrection. He knew that his momentary afflictions were just that—momentary. He didn't need more or want other things. His contentment was in knowing that there was a great reward to come. He was confident that Jesus would take care of him in the future. Thank God for what you have, and as you do, you will experience a new joy in each day.

Father, thank you for all that you have given me. Help me to be content with what I have.

PRAISE

Let everything that has breath
praise the LORD.
Praise the LORD.
PSALM 150:6 ESV

When you encounter a person whom you admire, perhaps an athlete, an artist, or someone very talented, how easy is it to say something good about them? It is not hard to praise them. Often when they are famous, throngs of people surround them. You may not even get close enough to say anything. Our motivation in this situation is usually selfish; we engage for our own gratification, in order to receive a response or to have something to boast about.

God, who is more famous, talented, and admirable than anyone, receives our praise directly. He also responds personally, and he wants us to boast all about how we know him. That's what it means to praise God. He wants us to tell everyone about what he has done. Praise him! The cool thing about praising God is that you can do it anywhere and at any time. He is constantly available to be praised.

God, I praise you! You are awesome! You are such a great father to me!

MODESTY

Put on then, as God's chosen ones, holy and beloved,
compassionate hearts, kindness, humility, meekness, and patience.
COLOSSIANS 3:12 ESV

People praised him for his words. He spoke with authority and clarity.
When he was sharing a story, a hush would fall, and people listened
intently. They would come up to him later and tell him how amazing
he was, how they were lost in what he was saying. His response, always
driven by meekness, was simple and humble. And he would often
encourage others in their gifts. People walked away from being with
him feeling lighter. They knew they were in the presence of an authentic,
unpretentious person who loved God and shared his gifts with them.

You can be a modest person. It takes humility and giving of yourself.
You just have to move away from promoting yourself and your
accomplishments. Then use your God-given gifts to serve others. As you
move yourself aside and allow God to speak and act through you, you
can show love with modesty.

*God, I know that I am awesomely made. You did that so I can serve others
and love them in the unique way you made me to. Help me to humbly love
well with the gifts you have given me.*

TRY TO FOLLOW

We continually ask God to fill you with the knowledge of his will through all the wisdom and understanding that the Spirit gives, so that you may live a life worthy of the Lord and please him in every way: bearing fruit in every good work, growing in the knowledge of God.

COLOSSIANS 1:9-10 NIV

Where does wisdom come from? It comes from the Holy Spirit. Worldly wisdom is not a complete waste; it just doesn't please God like the wisdom that comes from his Spirit does. Jesus said that God will use foolish things to confound the wise, and the weak things to shame the strong because those who are wise and strong think that they do not need God. Eventually our trust in ourselves leads us to distance ourselves from him. He knows this. It is why he rejects the proud but gives grace to the humble.

To gain wisdom, godly wisdom, you need to seek out his Spirit. How? Read the book of Proverbs and substitute the word, "wisdom," with the name, "Holy Spirit." It will give you insight. The Holy Spirit is sensitive to your sin and his presence in your life is not easily maintained. It requires you to sacrifice daily and to align yourself with Christ.

Holy Spirit, give me wisdom and patience as I try to follow your leading.

EXCEPTIONAL

David shepherded them with integrity of heart;
with skillful hands he led them.

PSALM 78:72 NIV

David was an exceptional shepherd. He killed a bear and a lion while protecting his flock. That was no small feat! He also didn't slack off. He worked with purpose and diligence in order to take care of his sheep. It is difficult to be truly exceptional. In school, students receive awards for exceptional work, extraordinary effort, and remarkable performances. But these seem to be handed out so flippantly today that we have lost the meaning of the word. If everybody is exceptional, nobody is. What does it mean to truly be brilliant and to display incomparable skills at a task? We are talking about humans who are in the top of their fields: Nobel peace prize winners, Olympic medalists, and other amazing achievers.

If he were on earth today, Jesus would be at the top of the heap when it comes to spiritual and human performance. He was astonishingly wise, extremely loving, and amazingly unique. His same Spirit dwells in you today. He makes you exceptional.

Jesus, you are awesome. Show me your ways so that I can imitate you.
I want to be amazing like you were when you walked the earth.

POLITE

Remind them to never tear down anyone with their words or quarrel,
but instead be considerate, humble, and courteous to everyone.
TITUS 3:2 TPT

Did you ever take a science class and have to calculate potential energy using an object's mass, gravity, and height? You may have done that this year. Few of us remember how to do those calculations after a few years because we don't use the formula in our daily lives. But when we learn what it means to be civil and how to be considerate of others, we do remember that. Why? Because encountering people is something we do every day. Additionally, remembering anything tied to emotions and having human interaction makes it much easier to recall. Our memories and emotions function from the same region of the brain.

Being polite is something God favors over being discourteous or argumentative. He wants you to represent him in the way you act and speak. In your hurried state, or sometimes just when you are annoyed, you likely speak out or act rudely. You can change this by going back to the basics, slowing down, and treating people with respect.

Jesus, help me to show respect to all people. Even in my busy and rushed moments, help me to be polite.

ULTIMATE ACHIEVEMENT

Patient endurance is what you need now,
so that you will continue to do God's will.
Then you will receive all that he has promised.

HEBREWS 10:36 NLT

It took thirty days broken up over seven years, usually between three and five hours at a time, sitting and waiting. Sometimes it was beautiful, and sometimes it was stormy, but most often it was cold, freezing cold. The best days boasted lots of activity. Birds flitted around in the trees. Squirrels hopped around hiding their winter bounty. The most incredible beauty was at the break of dawn or when the sun went sleepily to bed. Favorite moments occurred while listening to the snow fall. The air was so still you could hear the flakes land.

It was all about patience; quietly sitting and waiting; being still and listening. These were great moments to be with God. And all that waiting for all those years ended in a single moment. That was what it meant to be a hunter of white-tailed deer in the chilly Midwest. At first, it was laborious and difficult. The mind was often distracted and the body uncomfortable sitting for so long in one spot. But in the end, it was amazing to see what patience was obtained through practice and with a goal in mind.

God, help me to be patient and enduring in my faith. I want to receive all that you have promised.

READ

Faith comes by hearing,
and hearing by the word of God.
ROMANS 10:17 NKJV

When we read the Bible, we can quickly forget that it is a record of God's words. Men heard from God and wrote it down. We can "hear" the words of God by reading the Bible. If we apply this verse another way, we could say that faith comes by reading the Word of God. Everything in our faith is dependent upon understanding Scripture and appropriately applying it to our lives.

As we listen to the Holy Spirit, he speaks to us and affirms what the Bible says. It is through the Holy Spirit that God speaks to us personally. Keep listening for the Holy Spirit to speak to you especially as you read his Word. He loves to reveal Jesus as you do.

Holy Spirit, speak to me and open my eyes to Jesus. I want to know more about him and draw closer to him.

AFFIRMED

Today the LORD has proclaimed to you to be His special people,
just as He promised you, that you should keep all His commandments.
DEUTERONOMY 26:18 NKJV

Israel was chosen by God to be an example to the nations around them.
He gave them land, blessed them, and promised that if they followed his
law, they would dwell with eternal security with him in their midst. They
failed miserably, and he gave them over to the nations around them. They
have been an example of both mankind's failure and restoration. God
knew that they would fail, but that was not the complete story because
he had a plan through Christ. He used the law to demonstrate our
wickedness; with laws, we follow our own hearts.

Our hearts need healing before we can follow God's Spirit. Through Christ,
he healed us and wrote the law in our hearts. He filled us with his Spirit,
and now even those of us who are Gentiles can enjoy being chosen by him.
You are chosen by God. He loves you and calls you his special son.

Father, thank you for choosing me and making me a part of your family.

NEEDED

Some parts of the body that seem weakest and least important are actually the most necessary. So, God has put the body together such that extra honor and care are given to those parts that have less dignity. This makes for harmony among the members, so that all the members care for each other.

1 CORINTHIANS 12:24-25 NLT

As a family, in order to accomplish a task, we come together and utilize all of our gifts. It may be that we need to do springtime cleaning, a landscaping project, or a volunteer opportunity. In most cases, families know what skills each person has and how best to use them. But what happens when we want to include more relatives, like cousins, uncles, and aunts? Or maybe we've got a larger group that includes friends of friends? We get lost when we have too many people and we may end up telling them, "We don't need you for this." We are overwhelmed by the work of trying to include all those people.

God's level of inclusiveness is exclusive. It is astounding that he can take all parts of any society and all people groups and make them unified, cooperative, and functional. It is a societal miracle. Inside of that worldwide melting pot is you. You are needed. You are wanted by God for his purposes.

Thank you, God, for the gifts you have given me. Use them for your purposes and be honored by what I do for you.

RECEPTIVE

"Whoever welcomes this little child in my name welcomes me; and whoever welcomes me welcomes the one who sent me. For it is the one who is least among you all who is the greatest."

LUKE 9:48 NIV

Jesus was open to meeting with anyone, but he was specifically receptive to children, the poor, the oppressed, and the broken. Those society cast aside, he loved. He was interested in those who were lacking resources and relationships. This was not limited to the people we read about in the four gospels, for throughout the Bible God emphasizes this same level of care. In fact, it is the core of the gospel message over time.

God restores and those who are responsive to his openness receive everything he promises. When a human recognizes their true state before a holy and righteous God, there is a desperation to receive mercy and forgiveness. We are truly all in a state of poverty before him, and he is sympathetic toward us. He welcomes us like he does children. As God's child, you can be certain that he wants you to come to him as often as you want. He loves those who are humble and seek him.

Jesus, thank you for showing me the way to God. Help me to remain humble and to seek you often.

REFLECTIVE

By the grace given to me I say to everyone among you not to think of himself more highly than he ought to think, but to think with sober judgment, each according to the measure of faith that God has assigned.

ROMANS 12:3 ESV

The man looked in the mirror and pondered the wrinkles partially hidden by the stubble and the thinning, gray hair. It was no longer curly and had started to look scraggly. His eyes were still bright, and his heart was full of love, but his body was wearing away. What had he done with his life? What great thing had he accomplished? He was no saint, that was certain. Many of those wrinkles felt like deep reminders of his failures. Yet, that was the beauty of pondering this moment. Despite all the weighty issues, there was great life in him. His heart was full because of his relationships; his love was deep because of his Savior.

You will be like this man one day, thinking about who you have become and the victories and failures in your life. Set your heart and mind on Christ so that when that day comes, you can smile because of your deep love for your Savior.

Jesus, I want my life to be yours forever. Give me your strength to endure and to trust you always.

CHARITABLE

> "When you give to someone in need, don't do as the hypocrites do—blowing trumpets in the synagogues and streets to call attention to their acts of charity! I tell you the truth, they have received all the reward they will ever get."
>
> MATTHEW 6:2 NLT

Is it better to give than to receive? When we dwell on this, we may or may not recognize that we have been given so much already. Sometimes we think it would be better to receive, but we have been given so much that our lives should be about giving to others.

What have we been given? We have received forgiveness, salvation, a Christian family, unlimited grace, kindness, and faithful love. We have the Holy Spirit who fills us and overflows to others. He marks us for resurrection to an eternal, unblemished inheritance in Christ. This inheritance is life everlasting on a new earth with God dwelling among us. No more tears, pain, or sadness. You have all this and more from God. He has given you plenty so that you can give willingly to others.

I am thankful for what you have given to me, Jesus. Continue to show me all that you can do through me so that I am charitable toward others.

ENOUGH

Your unfailing love is better than life itself;
how I praise you!
I will praise you as long as I live,
lifting up my hands to you in prayer.
You satisfy me more than the richest feast.
I will praise you with songs of joy.

PSALM 63:3-5 NLT

It is common for us to want things to be easy. When we say this, we mean waking up not too early, doing productive things without trouble, and having good relationships with no drama. We want to enjoy life. But some philosophers believe that when life is too much like this, we go looking for trouble. We want to be challenged. If life is too sweet, we go looking for lemons. This is not far from the truth. We lack something that we cannot quite put our finger on. When is life enough? Our lack, or desire to mix it up, is the God-sized hole within each of us.

You will be satisfied when you find the place where God meets you. Excitement, peace, ease, and thrill all come together in a satisfying manner. God is more than enough for you.

God, show me how awesome you are. Help me to hunger and thirst for you, and to not chase other things that detract from your plan for me.

REST

> "My presence will go with you,
> and I will give you rest."
> EXODUS 33:14 ESV

What does it mean for you to rest? Most of us immediately think of the ways we relax. We take a break from our labor. But how often do we tie rest to the importance of taking time to stop and wait on God? When he speaks about being present with us and going with us in whatever we do, he is not talking about being inactive. He is talking about inviting him into what we are doing.

Resting in God is about acting while trusting him to be with us in what we do. It is a difficult task because we are typically self-reliant. He challenges us to learn how to request him to be a part of our everyday lives. When you make God a part of your day, he gives you the peace you need. What makes our days hard? Anxiety and worry certainly do. God promises that when he is with you, you can rest.

I trust in you, God. I ask that you would give me your peace and rest.

VALIDATED

Know this, my beloved brothers:
let every person be quick to hear, slow to speak.
JAMES 1:19 ESV

One of the hardest things for us to do is listen. In God's Word, especially as you read through the book of Proverbs, he compels us to be quiet and listen. When we listen well to people and we can respond with words that reflect to the speaker that we hear them properly, they feel validated and understood. It is not about being right or wrong; that is not the point. It is about making people feel heard. That is validation.

Our tendency is to move on from what someone is saying by forming arguments, trying to fix what is broken, or being distracted with our own thinking. It is important for us to learn the art of listening well, not just for the sake of others' validation, but also because it demonstrates maturity. We set ourselves aside in order to honor others. Isn't that what Jesus did? Take time when you are with your friends to listen, and not to speak. With your family, try waiting to hear their responses and then ask more questions. Learn how to listen and validate others.

Father, you are so good at listening to me and making me feel heard. Show me how to love others well by listening to them like you do for me.

RELATIONSHIP

The LORD is my strength and shield.
I trust him with all my heart.
He helps me, and my heart is filled with joy.
I burst out in songs of thanksgiving.

PSALM 28:7 NLT

When we have a friend we can count on, a friend who is always there, who supports us and gives good advice, it helps us feel secure. When we have a friend like this who is in a position of power and who doesn't care when or why we call because they just want to help, it gives us strength. And when we feel secure and strengthened by our relationships, we are filled with joy and thankfulness. This is what the author of this psalm is stating. He is close with God who is his companion in life.

You are able to have this same relationship with God. He is there for you in the same way. Rely on him and trust in him to take care of you.

Lord, I want to know you as my strength and my shield. I want to enjoy my relationship with you. Thank you for all that you have done and are doing in my life.

FRIENDS

Do not be deceived:
Evil company corrupts good habits.
1 CORINTHIANS 15:33 NKJV

At our age, we are less concerned with older generations. In fact, we often dismiss what they have to say, thinking that they are out of touch with our world. The reality is they are more in touch with it than we are. Our brains don't stop developing until we're twenty-five, and then we begin figuring out who we are. In the meantime, it is important for us to listen to the wisdom of those who have been through our stage of life. They are not deceived, and they can recognize how our friends influence us.

We are fully influenceable. We do things all the time to be funny, or cool, or just to fit in. We need to feel like we belong. This is normal and good, but we must make the effort to belong to good company. Think about your friend group. Do they pursue God, or do they chase after the world? Find friends that encourage your relationship with Jesus. Read the Word together and pray for each other. This pleases the heart of God.

Jesus, help me find friends that seek after you. And help me to not put as much time and energy into friends who do not.

NECESSARY

"Whenever you stand praying, forgive, if you have anything against anyone,
so that your Father also who is in heaven may forgive you your trespasses."
MARK 11:25 ESV

Jesus was hung up on forgiveness. Literally. He made it a must in our faith. It isn't optional; it's completely critical to the core of Christianity. How we practice forgiveness is a measure of how we will be forgiven. This is a condemning Word because we are broken beings and self-centered. We demand much of others and little of ourselves. We quarrel and fight because we do not have all that we want, and when we ask God for things, we often do so with the wrong motives.

We were friends of the world and enemies of God. Christ came to us, suffered, and died as one of us. He redeemed us and forgave us a debt we could never pay. So, he asks us to make sure we forgive others as he has forgiven us. *Wow.* If we put that into perspective, we would need to consider how many sins are mounted up against us, and then, hopefully, we choose to embrace the necessary practice of forgiveness. If you have people around you who have hurt you and you have not yet forgiven them, you must forgive. It is part of belonging to God's family. He forgave, so you can.

God, help me to forgive those who have sinned against me. Remind me of how much you have forgiven me.

PREPARED TO SURVIVE

Prepare your minds for action; discipline yourselves; set all your hope on the grace that Jesus Christ will bring you when he is revealed.

1 PETER 1:13 NRSV

The difference between being prepared or not can turn a simple weather situation into a life-or-death situation. If you have ever been caught in a storm where the temperature dropped suddenly and heavy rains and strong winds developed, you know what this means. The right equipment—usually an additional warm layer, wool socks, and rain gear—allows you to endure a storm without a problem. When you are exposed and unprepared, it becomes an issue of survival.

Our preparation is also important in our spiritual lives. How are we ready for what we may face when political climates change, or when people turn against Christians? We need to be prepared for all that is ahead of us. You can be prepared by spending time with God and following the guidelines he has laid out for you in his survival book—the Bible.

God, I want to be ready. I want to be prepared for action mentally, physically, and spiritually. Show me the best way to train and discipline myself to endure for your glory.

HE IS CLOSE

God is our refuge and strength,
A very ready help in trouble.
PSALM 46:1 NASB

Have you ever been in a situation when you had to call someone for help and as you went to call, your friend called you? Or perhaps you called one of your friends right when they needed it? It is one of those odd things that happen more often than people acknowledge. But is it really odd? We all have the ability to listen to God and act. At times he puts friends on our hearts, and when we respond, he uses that to encourage and strengthen them. God is a ready helper, and he is looking out for us much more than we may realize.

You have a refuge and strength in God. Though you may feel that he is sometimes absent, or distant, or unreachable, look around you and see how he has used your friends to touch your life. He is always with you, and he knows the best way for you to be encouraged. Have faith that he is faithful and ready to help you.

God, I believe that you are always present. Help me to see you in each day. I want to know that you are close by.

CLING

God is able to provide you with every blessing in abundance, so that by always
having enough of everything, you may share abundantly in every good work.

2 CORINTHIANS 9:8 NRSV

If someone did not know anything about God but they read the Bible and
studied God's deeds, and then they compared it to how Christians live,
would they wonder if God really saved us? Is he really enough? It doesn't
seem like Christians live like they have God's saving faith already.

God's salvation is complete. We cannot earn it more. Not only did he
provide salvation, but he also provides the means to live abundantly.
The issue is not his provision; it is our dependence. Do we live like we
need him? Who likes a desperate, clingy person? Most of us live without
desperation. Who wants to be desperate? There are times when we need
him, and he is faithfully there for us, but he wants us to get to a place of
needing him every day. God is looking around the world for people who
are sold out for him. He wants you to be so close that you cling to him.
Then he will use you in incredible ways for his kingdom.

*God, show me how to cling to you like I lost my footing and I'm holding
onto the face of a cliff just to survive.*

UNWAVERING

Flee youthful passions and pursue righteousness, faith, love, and peace,
along with those who call on the Lord from a pure heart.
2 TIMOTHY 2:22 ESV

He was determined to influence him. His best effort came when he asked him to stay overnight. His house was cool with cars, posters, videos, and other fun things to do. When his friend came over, he showed him his room. And that was the start of things falling apart. His buddy told him that if he wanted him to stay, he had to take down the poster of the topless girl. He did. When they went to watch a video, he pulled out something pornographic and his friend was stern. "If you put that on, I'll leave." All the things he thought were cool were not to this guy. What made him so unmovable? The boy had talked about Jesus, and as the weekend went on, he realized this kid was unwavering in his faith.

When you get ahold of Christ, you can be determined to keep him. But he actually keeps you. Your best efforts to remain in him involve staying separate from the world and free from the love of what it offers. Guard your faith with diligence.

Jesus, give me strength to leave behind what the world offers me and to chase after you.

DARING

Some trust in chariots and some in horses,
but we trust in the name of the LORD our God.
PSALM 20:7 NIV

The adolescent was cheered on by his classmates. In the back of their minds, they would never do what he was doing. Across the school and over a few fences were some horses. They dared him to get there and back before the teacher returned to class. What for? Was there some great reward? No. He was just full of courage, and maybe a little excited by adrenaline. Off he went as fast as he could. Across the sports fields, over the two fences. Then he slowed down, so as not to spook the horses. He bravely walked up to the biggest one and spoke softly, patting him on the head.

As soon as he had done so, a distant roar of celebration drifted to his ears. Lost in his own adventure, the sound sparked a memory, "My class and my teacher!" He turned and raced back. With sweat dripping down his forehead, and damp clothes, he valiantly opened the door with a broad smile to be met by the scowling teacher. You can be brave when cheered on by friends. How brave can you be when you know God is cheering you on?

God, I want to hear you daring me to do great things in your name. Give me ears to hear your Spirit speaking to me.

IT IS TODAY

Encourage one another daily, as long as it is called "Today,"
so that none of you may be hardened by sin's deceitfulness.
HEBREWS 3:13 NIV

This verse is important in highlighting how sin works in our hearts to
deceive us. When we give our lives to sin, we become more deceived.
What does that look like in our world? Think through society and what
is celebrated. Is marriage celebrated? Does the world ever set aside a day
to celebrate self-sacrificing people ? Not all of what society celebrates is
righteous and good. Some of it is.

Sin deceives; what is evil is called good, and what is good is called evil.
This is the danger of sin. The old adage about playing with fire and
getting burned comes to mind. In your heart, determine not to play with
the fire of sin. If you give your life to God and obey him by being with
other God-fearing people, you will not become deceived.

*God, I want your truth to lead me. Holy Spirit, help me to guard my heart
and to have friends who love you.*

WEALTH

Whoever is generous to the poor lends to the LORD,
and he will repay him for his deed.
PROVERBS 19:17 ESV

There are many verses in the Bible about wealth and poverty. It is one of the biggest issues that God has with men. Money is the cause of many evils in the world, and God makes us aware of this in his Word. He knows how easily our hearts become chained to the pursuit of wealth. What can we do to guard our hearts against the love of money and possessions? We can give generously and lend to others, and we can love others with our possessions. We can find ways to make our hearts trust God and not money.

God also loves the poor. His heart is for those who have needs but do not have all they require to meet those needs. He cares for those who are not just poor in their possessions, but also struggle emotionally, physically, and mentally. God cares more about these than any other. You and I should too.

God, I want to know your heart for those who are poor so that I do not become obsessed with my own wealth. Help me love those you love.

FEARLESS

"Fear not, for I am with you;
be not dismayed, for I am your God;
I will strengthen you, I will help you,
I will uphold you with my righteous right hand."

ISAIAH 41:10 ESV

If we take this word literally, there is not a fearless person among us. Those who have no fear take risks that could be dangerous or even fatal. Fear is healthy. Too much fear can disable you, but the right amount keeps you alive. Fear helps us restrain our actions and words. When we demonstrate courage, daring, and bravery, we overcome fear by choice. We look it in the eye and say, "Not this time, my friend. I have bold things to do."

God gives you the ability and the confidence to be fearless in the face of opposition. He tells you that he is with you. You don't need to be afraid; you can be courageous. In him lies the strength to step up in a situation. When you fall, he is there to catch you. He restores you in his love, and you are safe in him.

Father, I trust in you to keep me safe. I pray you would help me be wise and brave. I would like to do the things that you tell me to do and have the wisdom to know when it is not your voice that I am following.

GUARD YOUR HEART

"God so loved the world that He gave His only begotten Son,
that whoever believes in Him should not perish but have everlasting life."

JOHN 3:16 NKJV

You see it at sports games, on billboards, in the news, and on church pews. John 3:16 is the most recognized verse in the world today. Strangers to the Bible even recognize it but may not know what it refers to. They may think John was born March 16th. So? Who cares?! But no, this verse is a magnificent summary of God's love, the purpose of his Son, and the result he provides for all who believe.

If you keep reading, it also tells us that the result of those who do not believe is judgment for their sins. This is not something any of us want when we stand before God. If you believe in Jesus, follow him with all your heart. Strive to work out your salvation with fear and trembling so that you do not become one of those who have lost your belief in him. His work is complete. Now guard your heart and pursue him only.

Jesus, fuel my fire for you. Keep me safe and watch over me today. Help me to love you more.

TO BE UNDERSTOOD

If anyone sees a fellow believer in need and has the means to help him,
yet shows no pity and closes his heart against him,
how is it even possible that God's love lives in him?

1 JOHN 3:17 TPT

Compassion is a strength to those in need of it. It enables a hurting person to express what they feel freely and then to be understood. When we are understood, we can begin the process of healing. Jesus is compassionate. He connects with us on any level to grasp what we are experiencing and to feel what we feel. His tenderness toward us when we are in a place of brokenness or pain is strengthening.

What is also amazing about experiencing compassion and the comfort it brings is that we learn how to express thoughtful care toward others by how we have been treated in our own times of need. We can then comfort those who are suffering. God intends for you to experience comfort in him so that you can have compassion for others. He is not angry or vengeful. He is kind and merciful and wants you to be the same toward all you encounter.

Thank you for your kindness toward me, God. Give me your strength to love others in the same way.

PLEASURE FOREVER

"This is the confidence we have in approaching God:
that if we ask anything according to his will, he hears us."
JOHN 5:14 NIV

If your parents' desires were clear to you and you also wanted what they wanted, would it be hard for you to approach them and ask for it? No! This is the relationship God wants for all who are his children. He says that he knows what we need even before we ask, so we do not even need to worry about it. We can have confidence that when our hearts are aligned with his, what we want is what he wants.

This understanding should drive us to know him more! Seek God with all your heart. Find out what makes him pleased and run after those things. Turn away from what the world offers in terms of entertainment, possessions, and pleasure, as those are temporary. What God offers is eternal and that will bring total satisfaction.

God, I want what you want. But I know my heart loves the things the world offers. Protect me and give me the strength to follow you.

STAY AWAKE

"I say to everyone—
be awake at all times."
MARK 13:37 TPT

Jesus was suffering. He was about to go to the cross and he knew it. In the forefront of his mind was the separation from his Father that he was about to endure. This critical sacrifice happened as Jesus bore the sins of the world and died. God cannot have any relationship with our sin. He cannot be in the presence of sin. He is holy and righteous. So, he was pleased to punish Jesus for our sake as well as for the disciples' sake. Yet, they could not stay awake. He had to wake them up during the toughest time of his life.

We are like the disciples and fall asleep during our own walk with God. We are so often unaware of what is happening around us. You don't need to be stuck in your own thinking, unaware of the trouble in your life or in the lives of others around you. Your warrior King is calling you to be alert for what is happening in your world, to pray and to listen for his voice. Be alert at all times!

Jesus, you are awesome. You are a mighty warrior watching and protecting me. Help me to stand with you in battle and to be alert at all times. Keep me awake.

A GRAIN OF RICE

Do not neglect your gift…. Be diligent in these matters;
give yourself wholly to them, so that everyone may see your progress.

1 TIMOTHY 4:14-15 NIV

At certain fairs or events there are vendors who sell small trinkets. They make them onsite and often include your name on them. One particular vendor has the most painstakingly precise task to build their craft. Using a fine-tip pen, a magnifying device, and one grain of rice, they work hard to carefully create a personalized grain of rice that is then put into a tiny glass bottle and made into a necklace. Is it of such fine detail, that your vision would have to be perfect in order to read it without a magnifying lens.

What a skill! And how creative! When we are committed, hardworking, and industrious, there are few limits to what we can do. When we set our minds on a task and are intentional about completing it, we can perform amazing things. God made us to be creative and hardworking!

God, help me not to neglect the gifts that you have blessed me with. I want to work hard and be diligent. Show me how to run after the things that are on your heart for me to do.

DRIVEN

Without faith living within us it would be impossible to please God.
For we come to God in faith knowing that he is real
and that he rewards the faith of those who passionately seek him.
HEBREWS 11:6 TPT

His dad would take him to the auction, and they would drive several cars.
They would look them over, talk about them, and then even bid on one
once in a while. Was it the cars or the bidding wars that carried the most
excitement? It was a thrilling time in his childhood. Of course, growing
up in a family that loved cars meant he could not wait to be behind the
wheel of his own vehicle one day. It didn't matter what sort of car he
drove; he just wanted to be in control, punching the gas, gripping the
wheel, and shifting gears. His obsession propelled him to own a different
car every few years.

You have desires that help determine a path for your life. Sometimes
desires are realized, and other times they are fleeting, but you can be sure
you have a drive to do something. When you are not motivated, you will
end up drifting in life, and this can have negative consequences. God
desires for you to be fulfilled and focused.

*Jesus, I want my desires to be yours. I want to be driven by what drives you.
Put in my heart the desires of your heart and show me how to live as you
lived on this earth.*

CAPTURED

The Son is the radiance of God's glory and the exact representation of his being, sustaining all things by his powerful word. After he had provided purification for sins, he sat down at the right hand of the Majesty in heaven. So he became as much superior to the angels as the name he has inherited is superior to theirs.

HEBREWS 1:3-4 NIV

Have you ever been so engrossed in something that you didn't notice what was happening around you? People have accidents all the time because of this. It can be as small an issue as knocking over a drink to something huge like crashing a car or even harming someone. When something has taken ahold of our attention, we are no longer "of this world." We are mesmerized by what we are engaged in.

God would love for you to be this way with him: that you would find that place where you love being in his presence and delight in him to the fullest. All you need to do is work on going deeper in God.

God, I know you can capture my imagination and fill my heart with desire for you. Show me how to live so that my life is joined to yours.

CONTROL

Refrain from anger, and forsake wrath!
Fret not yourself; it tends only to evil.
PSALM 37:8 ESV

He was at a point of meltdown. He was going to meet a friend in another state and was running late to the airport. Check-in and security took way too long, and he moved as fast as he could with bags banging against his legs. When he arrived with sweat dripping down his back, he found the boarding door was shut, and he watched the jetway pull back from the plane. He banged angrily on the door, all balance and reason flushed away. He yelled like a toddler, screaming at the door. But it was to no avail. It lasted for a few minutes; obscenities, fears, and overreactive emotions all burst forth with no logical reason. Rationality returned when he calmed down. Reality sunk in and he realized that he had an audience. Shame crept over him. Silently he sat and fumed.

It is not fun when your brain becomes unbalanced. When you lose control, the animal part of your brain can begin to drive your emotions. Rational thinking flies out the window. This is where your good God has given the Holy Spirit to be with you, and to aid you in self-control and patience.

Holy Spirit, help me to be controlled. When I am angry, show me how to stay away from sinning. Teach me to calm down quickly and use my brain to think through a situation rather than react emotionally.

HATED FIRST

"If the world hates you, know that it has hated me before it hated you. If you were of the world, the world would love you as its own; but because you are not of the world, but I chose you out of the world, therefore the world hates you."

JOHN 15:18-19 ESV

It is difficult to live apart from this world. Really hard. The world offers so much, and it is easy to access. There are many people who love the things of the world, so there is a lot of pressure to love the world too. However, Jesus made it clear that if we are to be a part of his kingdom, we are not to be like the world. We have to choose to not love things that seem easy to love. And we must love things that are hard to obtain. Delighting in God is not for the faint hearted. It is for the brave, the diligent, and the persevering souls who do not cower in corners. It is for those who stand in the face of hate and say yes to Jesus.

You are choosing to love Jesus. You are not alone. He is with you, and there are others who are in the same position as you. Look beyond the popular people in this world and find friends within the brave men and women of faith. They are the ones you need to be with.

Father, thank you for the strength to love you. Help me to be with those you love and to love you more than I love the things of the world.

CLOSER

A soft answer turns away wrath,
But a harsh word stirs up anger.
PROVERBS 15:1 NKJV

It is easy for us to be rude to someone who was rude to us. We don't have to think about it. It comes out as fast as they can dish it. But is that the way God wants us to be? No. He asks us to be like him. We sin all the time against him, yet he still encourages us to come to him humbly, and he always wants a relationship with us. He could be angry, yet he responds with kindness. He could destroy us with one word, yet he has mercy. This is why he tells us to forgive and love others. He provides the Holy Spirit to help us. He knows that on our own we cannot do this.

You do not need to strive to be Jesus. Tell him how weak you are at being like him on your own. Embrace his kindness and his mercy and it will help you be more like him. Ask the Holy Spirit to guide your steps and your words.

Thank you, Jesus, for the Holy Spirit who helps me. Guide my steps and my words and draw me closer to you each day.

WALK AND TALK

Rejoice always, pray without ceasing, give thanks in all circumstances;
for this is the will of God in Christ Jesus for you.
1 THESSALONIANS 5:16-18 ESV

Have you ever been able to do something for a whole day without being interrupted ? Not likely. When Paul wrote about praying without ceasing, could he have meant it literally, and if so, how would anyone get anything done? We know for a fact that Paul did much more than just pray all the time. He was a traveling missionary who mostly supported himself by working each place he stayed. He would often be engaged in discussions at the synagogues and with city elders. He spread the Word of God to people constantly. There is no way he wanted us to stop doing life in order to pray.

So, what did he mean? He is encouraging you to live in a spirit of prayer, and to walk as though Christ is next to you, sharing your life with you. When your thoughts are conversations with God, all of sudden you become a walking prayer. That is what is means to be a truly prayerful person.

Jesus, I want to walk and talk with you. If I do, I know that my life will be better aligned with your will.

CELEBRATED

Celebrate with praises the God and Father of our Lord Jesus Christ, who has shown us his extravagant mercy. For his fountain of mercy has given us a new life—we are reborn to experience a living, energetic hope through the resurrection of Jesus Christ from the dead.

1 PETER 1:3 TPT

Life is worth celebrating. It is precious. When a couple finds out they are expecting a baby, there are many emotions experienced. This surprising bit of news can be delightful or perhaps even scary. But whatever other emotions are experienced upon hearing the news, the day of the baby's birth, and each year's birthday after that, the child is celebrated. It is because we value life. And the things we value are the things we typically celebrate.

We celebrate new life, beautiful beginnings, holidays, fresh creativity. In these seasons of life, it feels good to be alive. Whether it is the start of something new or the achievement of a goal, when we celebrate, it is done best with others. That is the greatest way to enjoy the special occasion. It reminds us of our created purpose to enjoy all that God has blessed us with. Get together with friends who love God and celebrate your friendships. Remind your friends of the good things God has done for all of you.

God, help me encourage my friends with reminders of your mercy and the new life that you have given each of us.

GIVE THANKS

Give thanks for everything to God the Father
in the name of our Lord Jesus Christ.
EPHESIANS 5:20 NLT

The family struggled each month to live on their low income. It was difficult with four jobs between the two adults, but they worked hard and budgeted carefully. They shopped clearance sales for clothing, discount stores for groceries, and garage sales for their home furnishings. They used the rest of their money to give to others and to enjoy a family event once a month. With smart management and shrewd actions, they were even able to save a bit. After years of living carefully within their means and multiplying what little they had, they were able to purchase a property, and then another, and yet another until they owned many properties. They used these many properties to bless others beyond what they could ever have imagined.

When you are wise about how you live and you honor God with your finances, he can use you to bless others far more than what you could have seen or imagined. At the core of this is being thankful and grateful for what you have now. Love what you have, and you will be content.

God, thank you for all that you have given me. Help me to be grateful for what I have. I want to have a thankful heart.

TO LOVE OTHERS

Most important of all,
continue to show deep love for each other,
for love covers a multitude of sins.

1 Peter 4:8 nlt

It started with Jesus. He loved us so much that he left heaven and came down to earth. God himself became a dependent baby, suffered immensely, and then finally died. He did all this to cover our sins. But he didn't stop there. Jesus continues to pray for us and extend forgiveness each day. He covers us with his love. *Wow*. Let that sink into your heart.

How must we act in light of this constant love? The Spirit asks that we love each other enough to cover the sins we commit when we hurt each other. How often do we complain about the little things that people do that we find annoying? Jesus encourages us to let those things go and just love each other. We need to not be so full of negativity, harboring our hurt. You can love others and cover their sin against you with God's love. It is not by your strength though. You must understand what God has done for you so that you can do the same for others.

Jesus, help me to know the strength of your love for me so that I can love others in the same way.

HUNGRY

Do not love the world or the things in the world. If anyone loves the world, the love of the Father is not in him. For all that is in the world—the desires of the flesh and the desires of the eyes and pride of life—is not from the Father but is from the world. And the world is passing away along with its desires, but whoever does the will of God abides forever.

1 JOHN 2:15-17 ESV

John writes of three things here that are not from the Father but create inappropriate wants and desires in us. Desires of the flesh are our urgings and yearnings. Desires of the eyes are the wanting and coveting what we should not have. And the pride of life feeds our over-inflated egos and our need for control.

You are troubled by these same cravings, yet God has delivered you from being a slave to them. You no longer walk around blind to your wrongful desires but are awakened by his Spirit. You have always been wanted by God, and now he places in you a new desire to want him. It is a marvelous change that has occurred. Be hungry for God.

God, teach me how to set aside the desires that are not of you. I want to pursue you.

COMPANION

The temptations in your life are no different from what others experience. And God is faithful. He will not allow the temptation to be more than you can stand. When you are tempted, he will show you a way out so that you can endure.
1 CORINTHIANS 10:13 NLT

It is said that good timing is everything. If you play sports, you know that timing is critical to making a play. Whether you're passing the ball to a receiver, or you're swinging the bat at a pitch, the appropriate timing results in a positive play. Delays in a race put you in a tough spot if you hope to win. If you play an instrument and your timing is off, the performance is disrupted. Being late to class or to work is not fitting and can result in disciplinary action. Similarly, God has timing in all things. Good timing.

Keep God in your mind as you are in his. He promises to be with you when you put him first, and when you do, you will escape every temptation and trial.

God, I can trust in you. I want to see you moving in my life. Help me to know you are with me. Give me your wisdom so I can overcome temptation.

NO COMPARISON

"You must not covet your neighbor's house.
You must not covet your neighbor's wife, male or female servant,
ox or donkey, or anything else that belongs to your neighbor."
EXODUS 20:17 NLT

The enemy of contentment is comparison. It is hard not to compare when you see that sweet ride drive by, a luxurious home, or that beautiful girlfriend. None of them are ours, but we want them anyway. Comparison is the culprit. If most of us were thankful for what we had, what we had would be enough. That is the key to sufficiency—thankfulness.

When we dive into comparison, we sin by coveting, and then we attempt to find replacements for our dissatisfaction with other things. We need to turn to God and tell him how we feel and what we want. This is not so that he gives us everything, but he does listen, and he wants to speak to us. God wants you to understand that all he has given you is adequate. He wants to turn your heart to him and away from distractions. What you have is sufficient and you only need to look to him.

Father, you have given me so much more than I deserve. Most of all, I am thankful for the gift of eternal life that you have given me.

QUIET

I am standing in absolute stillness, silent before the one I love,
waiting as long as it takes for him to rescue me.
Only God is my Savior, and he will not fail me.
PSALM 62:5 TPT

Have you ever been by the water alone and the waves are gently lapping the shore? Or have you walked in the woods with a light breeze blowing but not a sound otherwise can be heard? Have you stood on a mountain top and gazed out over the valley, not seeing any other person? These are places of real stillness and quiet. It's so silent that the sound of the leaves rustling in a light breeze or the water rippling in a brook can be heard.

Sometimes you can find these moments of quiet in a cabin by the lake or in an empty park. It is hard to find them in the electronically stimulated homes that always seem to be abuzz. These places are so still you can hear your own breathing and your heart beating. God loves to be in those still, quiet places with you. It is there that you can also hear his heartbeat.

God, I want to know what your heart beats for. Help me to get away from the busy noises in order to sit with you and listen.

ADORATION

How right they are to adore you.
SONG OF SOLOMON 1:4 NLT

He was a young boy when he first watched a jet fly by overhead. His attention was drawn by the sound, and then by the intrigue as he watched it fly away. The streaks in the sky reminded him of toy cars leaving trails in the sand, or paths of footprints in the plush carpet at Grandma's house. As he grew, his passion for flying increased. He traveled the world with his family, and each time he walked past the cockpit of the plane, he peered in. The dials and knobs intrigued him. His first computer was quickly loaded with fighter pilot games and flying simulators. As he explored the world before him, twisting and turning in dogfights with the enemy, his admiration for flying grew. Late in the night, under a dimly lit poster of an old F-16, he would fall asleep, exhausted from the battles. Soon his devotion earned him a place in the Air Force and then a graduate degree. It was not long after that his affection for fighters was realized and he became the man streaking the sky with his trails, soaring with sound, and awakening adoration in the next generation.

You have things that capture your imagination and drive your passions. God wants you to realize how amazing he is. He can be your greatest passion.

God, help me to learn what it looks like to adore you, to be passionate about who you are, and how we can work together to do all you want to do in my life.

ADRENALINE JUNKIE

Don't act thoughtlessly,
but understand what the Lord wants you to do.
EPHESIANS 5:17 NLT

What gets you excited? When your imagination and memory come together to recreate experiences that are full of fun, joy, passion, thrill, or intensity, what do you picture? It could be a concert, a sporting event, a particular person or group of people, or an experience. Sometimes it's all of those. We have many avenues for excitement in life, and some people seek thrills without rest. We call these people adrenaline junkies. They live for the next high which can be dangerous. When they come down from that high, they risk crashing.

It places an unusual strain on the body to live in constant excitement and the search for it because it was not what God intended for us. God does want you to be excited about him though. He wants you to enjoy his creation too. But he has so much more for you. The most satisfying excitement, the kind that lasts longer, comes when you encounter his Spirit. When you do, you can become more addicted to him!

God, I want to encounter your Spirit in a greater way. Please get me excited about the things you do and who you are!

SPLENDID

Splendid and majestic is His work,
And His righteousness endures forever.
PSALM 111:3 NASB

You may think of a sugar substitute when you read this word. Those little sugar replacement packets that are fake sweetness. But splendid means excellent, magnificent, luxurious, grand, elegant, or stylish. It is not often used, but when we consider its meaning, it brings to mind the ritzy hotel that few can afford to stay in, or the car that only the rich can drive, or the large homes on the cliff that movie stars live in. Basically, as an adjective, few can afford the splendid things in this life.

That is what is so great about God. He is splendid. He is magnificent. He is grand. And he is available to all of us. You have a father who gives good gifts, is generous, and who loves you. And you have an inheritance so perfect that you cannot comprehend it; it is glorious beyond your imagination. It is splendid and it will be yours to enjoy one day.

Father, you have great things in store for me. Remind me today of how splendid you are. Show me in your creation the magnificent things that you have made for me to enjoy.

INCONVENIENT

Do nothing from selfish ambition or conceit,
but in humility count others more significant than yourselves.
PHILIPPIANS 2:3 ESV

Paul wrote to the church in Philippi encouraging them to love one another. Soon after that, he encouraged them to have the same attitude as Christ did, who was God but chose to become a man. He made himself less in order to love us more. In a like manner, we are to empty ourselves and become like servants to one another. We see a form of this love where one lays down everything for another in young romance. People fall over themselves in order to dote on their love interest. Some of your friends may be in love like this. You may sometimes ask them why they are giving up everything to be with this other person. But this infatuation is fleeting. It is a temporary love. The love that Christ wants us to have for each other is permanent, pure, and self-sacrificing.

Jesus wants you to love your family in this way. He wants you to serve them when it is inconvenient and to look for ways to help them when you don't want to. As you practice loving them, you can then learn how to love people other than your family with the love of Jesus.

Jesus, help me to love my family well. Show me how to set my interests aside in order to care for them.

INFORMER

Do not keep talking so proudly or let your mouth speak such arrogance,
for the LORD is a God who knows, and by him deeds are weighed.

1 SAMUEL 2:3 NIV

The word *informer* brings to mind old war movies where people are
hiding, and the informers are out there in force. They have the power
and the information that will impact both their lives and those who are
hiding. Like in the Scripture above, they walk proudly, but they do not
realize that God watches their deeds. They may have temporary power
with their knowledge, but it is just that— temporary.

Knowledge is power. It enables a person to inform the uninformed. With
it they can appear to be confident and conversational. But because of its
impersonal nature, knowledge can lead to pride, so we must be careful.
Paul writes that knowledge puffs up a man, but love builds him up. He
encourages you to be informed when it comes to the nature and person
of Christ. He prays many times that you would know and understand
who God is and be filled with the knowledge of Jesus Christ—a
knowledge that is relational.

*God, I want my life to be filled with knowledge of you. Help me to spend
time growing in my relationship with you.*

TAKE CARE OF EVERYTHING

The generous man will be prosperous,
And one who gives others plenty of water will himself be given plenty.
PROVERBS 11:25 NASB

The generous bachelor grew up in a simple countryside town. He was independently successful and quite the catch for any girl. However, his true passion was to care for his family and those he was responsible for. He spent days traveling and helping people. Like a seasoned teacher, he spoke wise words for those who wanted to hear them. People marveled at his giving heart; he shared his time, resources, and talent with them. When he left a city, the place was abuzz with recollections about his actions. The crazy thing was that he never asked for anything in return except a genuine relationship. His words were a simple call. "Follow me."

Jesus is the truly giving man. When he walked the earth, he discipled with care, kindness, compassion, and sacrifice. He didn't need what others had because the Father took care of everything he needed. You can trust God to provide for all your needs so that you can give willingly and freely to those around you.

Jesus, like you, I want to be giving. Show me how to use my time, resources, and talents for your kingdom.

JUST AS JESUS DID

The wisdom that comes from God is first of all pure, then peaceful, gentle,
and easy to please. This wisdom is always ready to help those who are troubled
and to do good for others. It is always fair and honest.

JAMES 3:17 NCV

Reasonable people can logically follow sound thinking and understand how to grasp a process or its instructions. Their emotional state is balanced, and they know what others are experiencing. Have you tried to talk with someone who is unreasonable? Their emotions take over their responses. Their thoughts cannot process without tons of emotional baggage clouding their judgment. They end up answering with illogical, unrealistic, irrational statements that are often mixed with overly expressive words.

We have witnessed these people from various countries, genders, and ages. It's *that person* on all the media we have watched. Is there any sense trying to talk with them or even trying to help them? Yes, but it requires a reasonable and patient person to do so. You can help any unreasonable person just as Jesus did, and it would be considered part of your ministry to do so. Be patient, speak gently, and understand their situation. Someday you may be that person, and you will need a patient helper to level your thoughts.

Jesus, give me your wisdom in all situations. I know there will be some discussions when I just need to walk away and others when you can use me to help someone.

DECEMBER 7

AMAZING

When the crowd saw this, they were filled with awe;
and they praised God, who had given such authority to man.
MATTHEW 9:7-8 NIV

As they climbed the many steps, thoughts came to mind of the multitudes of people who had climbed there before them. How many people had walked here before? How many different ethnicities? The steps were worn in places where others had consistently walked. It was a sure sign that millions had been here before. And no wonder. It was an amazing feat of human engineering and work. The wall was up to eight meters in height and over five meters thick at the top in some sections. It could be seen from the moon! When they reached a high point, they stopped and turned to look out over the incredible view of mountains and valleys with beauty all around.

If we think humanity is somehow limited, it only takes a visit to the Great Wall of China to experience unbounded human power in creativity. Combine that with seeing it from space. These two awe-inspiring moments come together in one beautiful experience of ancient engineering and modern space travel. We see the incredible creation God made in humans and what we are capable of doing. God also made you to do incredible things. Align your heart with his and watch what happens!

God, help me to know your heart and act on it. I want you to do amazing things through me.

DECEMBER 8

SHREWD

Go to the ant, you sluggard;
consider its ways and be wise!
It has no commander,
no overseer or ruler,
yet it stores its provisions in summer
and gathers its food at harvest.

PROVERBS 6:6-8 NIV

Do you think of the ant as insightful and wise? Perhaps not quite. It seems they are preprogrammed to do what God made them do. That may be the point though. God made ants to do certain tasks, and he is telling the lazy man, "I didn't make you for this. Get up now and do the things I made you for!"

God put us to work when he created us. Man named the animals and was involved in that part of the creative process. We were commanded to take care of the earth and were given rulership over the whole domain. There is nothing about work that is wrong or evil. It is partially what we are made to do. But making it our number one priority or shirking it are both ungodly. God does not want you to sit around and be entertained. He made you to do things, to accomplish both your daily work as well as godly things for him. Make yourself busy with the things that he wants you to do.

God, help me to not be lazy but to work hard and enjoy the benefits of my labor.

PART OF HIS STORY

According to his promise we are waiting for new heavens
and a new earth in which righteousness dwells.

2 PETER 3:13 ESV

The old boat was haggard. Paint was chipping, some oarlocks were broken, a few of the floorboards were cracked, and the hull had a few leaks. The prow was the worst as it had taken a beating on the rocks over the years. It was going to be a long and hard task to rebuild her. Slowly and intentionally, week after week, the builder worked, starting with the prow, and then moving on. The final day of restoration came. The old had become new. Full of history and ready to write some more exciting stories, she slipped into the ocean with the family aboard.

God will restore the earth and will raise us up as a new creation. Our bodies will be restored, holding our histories but ready to write more. You are a part of God's story; you are making history as you live your life. Watch how you live and be intentional about what you do, remembering that God has a new heaven and new earth waiting for you.

Jesus, I want to live like you, making a difference in people's lives and helping others to know about the kingdom you are preparing for us.

SECRET DOOR

"You will seek me and find me,
when you seek me with all your heart."
JEREMIAH 29:13 ESV

Have you ever played a game where you have to collect certain articles or words of a phrase to open a secret door? Maybe you have read a book or watched a movie like this. The character works hard to search for clues in order to unlock and open the door. Fighting battles, growing skills, and developing knowledge, they arrive back at the door with all that they need to open it. They are sure it will lead to great rewards, and often the hardest door with the most risk to obtain the keys has the most reward to give.

God is very much like that door. He is easy to reach, to touch, and to know, but to get to his treasures, to go deep into his vault, you must venture into difficult territory. You have to take great risk, and likely experience great loss, but the reward of opening up who he is will completely astound you. Venture forth and find those lost items. Obtain your entry into his secret lair of goodness!

God, show me your great treasures! Give me the strength to keep searching until I find the way to your heart.

STRONG BUT GENTLE

May you always be filled with the fruit of your salvation—
the righteous character produced in your life by Jesus Christ—
for this will bring much glory and praise to God.
PHILIPPIANS 1:11 NLT

There is something pleasant about gentleness. It's the look of a mother holding a newborn babe, a father helping his child up from a fall, or the face of Jesus as he held out his hand to the woman caught in her sin. These are all pictures of gentleness in action. It is the kind, calming act that soothes and helps us in a time of difficulty.

For males, the concept of being gentle may be contradictory to what is traditionally considered manly. Men are supposed to be rough and hardy. But the truth is that real men know how to be gentle. A mature man can demonstrate ruggedness and tenderness. He can meet the needs of those around him not based upon his needs but upon his character. That is what we witness in the person of Jesus. What does it look like for you to be gentle? How can you show that to your friends and family?

Jesus, teach me how to be gentle as you were. Give me your wisdom to know when to be strong and when to be gentle.

FOR REAL

Unlike so many, we do not peddle the word of God for profit. On the contrary,
in Christ we speak before God with sincerity, as those sent from God.
2 CORINTHIANS 2:17 NIV

It's the look in their eyes. You think to yourself, *Are they for real?* Then
you see it. Yes, they are sincere. What is it about facial expressions and
human body language that helps us to communicate? When it comes to
interpersonal communication and the interaction between two people,
only seven percent of what we express is through words. The rest of it is
in tone of voice and body language. So, for sincerity, or humor, or anger,
or any emotion, much of what we hear and understand is seen through
our eyes and filtered through our previous experiences. Think of the
angry parent or the happy friend. We read much of what they express
in their body language. Sincerity is seen in an honest face with a candid
and genuine expression. Try to imagine Jesus holding out a hand toward
you. He is truthful and heartfelt in his love and care for you. There is no
trickery or scheming behind his eyes. He loves you sincerely.

*Jesus, I can trust you and your love for me. Thank you for your true
expression of love and kindness toward me.*

NOT BORING OR HARSH

I realize that the best thing for them is to be happy and enjoy themselves as long
as they live. God wants all people to eat and drink and be happy in their work,
which are gifts from God.

ECCLESIASTES 3:12-13 NCV

It has all come down to this—a final play. Our bodies are tense no matter
what side we are on. Adrenaline has been building up all through the
game to the point where we almost have headaches. "Come on, guys!
Win this thing!"

What is it about sports that gets us so excited? When your team wins
or even when it just makes a great play to get to the next level, there is
jumping, shouting, pumping fists in the air, clapping, and whooping. Is it
the release of all the stress, the joy of the win, or something more? God
must have a hearty laugh at our joy and celebration when our team wins.
He looks down and pats us on the back as if to say, "Wasn't that fun,
Son?" God loves seeing you animated and lively. You are his creation, and
he delights in seeing your enjoyment.

*God, sorry if I thought you were boring and harsh. You made me to enjoy
things, and you filled me with laughter and fun. Help me to remember that
even in the tough times in my life.*

POWER AND LIGHT

"I am the sprouting vine and you're my branches. As you live in union with me
as your source, fruitfulness will stream from within you—but when you live
separated from me you are powerless."

JOHN 15:5 TPT

Christmas is a great season for feeling connected to family especially when you set up the Christmas decorations. That arduous work of hanging lights, connecting wires, covering trees, bushes, and trim has to be completed first. It can be enjoyable when you do it together. But the real satisfaction comes when you connect everything and turn the lights on. Once connected to the power, everything lights up and brings great joy. There's a sense of satisfaction at what has been created. It doesn't seem to get old either. You can have the same set up for years and there is continued pleasure.

This is no different when we really connect with God. Things light up in our life. And each time we reconnect with him, there are similar emotions that bring a sense of joy and pleasure. You were made to be in a relationship with God. He wants to connect with you today and bless you with his power and light!

God, I want to connect with you. Power me up and help me today as I go about my plans.

EARTHQUAKE

*Be steadfast, immovable, always abounding in the work of the Lord,
knowing that in the Lord your labor is not in vain.*
1 CORINTHIANS 15:58 ESV

Have you ever been in an earthquake? The whole earth and everything
on it literally shakes. It's an apt name. It is also terrifying because there is
nothing to hold onto that is stable. Everything is moving; nothing is still.
What you think is stable could collapse. It is a chaotic experience that no
one should have to go through. The devastation created by a high scale
earthquake is horrific. Nothing is left standing.

God remains steadfast through the worst tragedies and disasters. He is
unshakable. His love for us is enduring, and his care for us is resolute. He
will not take his eyes off us; though we go through suffering and loss, he
is there, present and comforting. His promises will not fail. Though the
earth may groan, and people curse his name, Jesus will return and make
all things new. He is our unshakable hope. You can trust God to be there
through every shaky time in your life. He is a stabilizing force who will
never leave you or forsake you.

*I am so thankful for your strong love, God. Help me to trust in you alone
through my good and bad times.*

LISTEN AND OBEY

Don't just listen to God's word. You must do what it says.
Otherwise, you are only fooling yourselves.

JAMES 1:22 NLT

He heard, but he didn't want to do what he was being told to do. He kept running on ahead of his dad. It was not a safe path that they were on. There were dangers all around, but he wanted to prove that he could do it on his own. Sadly, he was only fooling himself. He kept going despite hearing the words from his dad. A root stuck up and tripped him. He fell, rolling down the cliff side, hitting rocks and breaking a rib. The sound of his father's words echoed in his mind. Laying at the bottom, pain stressing his body, he thought, "Why didn't I just listen and do what he said? Now our trip is ruined."

You can run ahead of God and try to prove yourself. He is patient, and he will pick you up when you fall. But remember your life will always go much better when you listen and obey him.

God, you are wise, and you care for me. Help me to not only read your Word and listen to your Spirit, but to also obey what you ask of me.

DECEMBER 17

YOUR DEVOTION

All the people were amazed and said,
"Perhaps this man is the Son of David!"
MATTHEW 12:23 NCV

Jesus was a miracle worker. That creates wonderment in all of us.
If you have seen a miracle—an unexplainable experience of divine
intervention—the astonishment lasts for a while. In Jesus' day, those
around him were talking about the things he did for weeks afterward.
They were considering who he was and then sharing his miracles with
others. Who was he, and why did he wield such power? He was the Son
of David, God in flesh, the Messiah!

Nowadays, his miracles would be splashed all over the globe. People
would be watching them on social media astounded by what he could do.
Others would still doubt him, thinking he was performing magic tricks.
But he is amazing; this is who he is. Jesus has not changed in his person
or his power. He has placed within you the same miraculous power of his
Spirit. The Holy Spirit can take your devotion and your gifts for God and
use them to demonstrate divine intervention.

*God, use me to do your work on earth. Help me devote my life to you so
that I am a trustworthy son, full of your Spirit's power.*

LIVE TO GIVE

God has proved his love by giving us his greatest treasure, the gift of his Son.
And since God freely offered him up as the sacrifice for us all,
he certainly won't withhold from us anything else he has to give.
ROMANS 8:32 TPT

Jesus was born in a manger in the town of Bethlehem with animals and shepherds all around him. The Creator became human and was also born into poverty. With no riches or glory, he was surrounded by lowly shepherds and their animals. The greatest gift to humanity was given to the least, and he lived his life to serve them. He spent his time with mostly outcasts and people of low status.

You have been given an extravagant gift. You have within you the same Spirit that was in Christ Jesus. The resurrection power of Christ lives in you! He is the assurance of your salvation and the mark that says you belong to God. Give to others what you have been given and share God's love.

Jesus, I want to learn how to live to give as you did. Help me to be filled with your Spirit so that I can pour out your love to others.

VALUED LIKE GOLD

More than that, I regard everything as loss because of the surpassing value of knowing Christ Jesus my Lord. For his sake I have suffered the loss of all things, and I regard them as rubbish, in order that I may gain Christ and be found in him.

PHILIPPIANS 3:8-9 NRSV

How do we attribute value to something? Think of gold and ask yourself why we value that metal over, say, iron ore. What about the value we give to diamonds over regular pebbles? Is it not because of the work involved in obtaining it or its scarcity amongst other, more common rocks and minerals? Our work and toil to produce gold and diamonds has come at a great cost to humanity over the years. Today many of the processes to produce these precious valuables are done with machines that ultimately save lives.

We place importance and value on things that deserve them. God says that he keeps himself hidden for those who seek him out. Like finding gold or diamonds, it takes work to build a relationship with him. This is not because he wants to play hard to get but because he wants us to value what we find and to treat it preciously. When you value something, you protect and keep it safe. Value your relationship with God.

God, I choose to protect my relationship with you. Show me how to do that so I always make you my greatest treasure.

SHARPSHOOTER

As you excel in everything—in faith, in speech, in knowledge, in all earnestness, and in our love for you—see that you excel in this act of grace also.
2 Corinthians 8:7 esv

He was a talented killer. He was a sharpshooter, and it never took him long to get his prey. He would set up his victim, obtain his sight lines. Once he was ready, he would push his tongue to the roof of his mouth, rapidly compress his gills, and shoot. Water would fly out like a jet stream and hit the victim in midair, mere feet away. His practiced precision made him proficient. One gulp and down it went. If you were not ready, it would all be over before you blinked an eye.

This amazing creature, called an archer fish, was made by God. He also made you, not as a bug killer, but as one who excels in the way he designed you to. So much of your body is well made, but he wants you to also be skilled in what you do, to be excellent at it.

I admire the way you created things, God. You are intelligent in your design. Help me to use the gifts and skills you have given me for your kingdom.

YOU ARE THANKFUL

The message of the cross is foolishness to those who are perishing,
but to us who are being saved it is the power of God.
1 CORINTHIANS 1:18 NKJV

It was not very loud, but he heard it. There was a muffled cry for help. He quickly scanned the water but couldn't tell where it was coming from. Then people started pointing. Without hesitation, he ran toward the noise. He dove in with a torrent of splashing water and swam hard. He reached the boy and before long both of them were safe and walking out of the ocean. The boy was exhausted but very thankful. The boy's family kept thanking the man over and over again. He didn't really know what to say. Language was a barrier. He just pointed to the son and told the family to make sure he got rest and care.

Being saved truly makes one thankful, and those in close relationships with the saved person are thankful too. Whether you are saved from drowning, an addiction, an accident, or anything else that could lead to death, there is a level of inexpressible gratitude felt by all. When you consider that Christ died to pay for your death, it is likely that you are thankful. His act to save you fills your heart with gratitude. Show him your appreciation in this season of giving by remembering his sacrifice and thanking him for it.

Jesus, thank you for coming to earth and sacrificing so much to save my life.
I love you.

MAN OF VALOR

Thank God! He gives us victory over sin and death
through our Lord Jesus Christ.
1 CORINTHIANS 15:57 NLT

Do we know what it means to truly be a victor? We play miniature games competing against each other in sports: basketball, tennis, golf, or perhaps a card game or a board game. But the truly triumphant ones are glorious battle-hardened men of valor. They understand not only the thrill of victory but also the sacrifices necessary to get there. True victors in battle have paid a great cost. They know what it means to lay down their lives for a cause and to exult when they overcome and win. That is real triumph.

Jesus is the final victor. He shares with us the blessings, knowing that we too have overcome and sacrificed to do so. But the glory ultimately goes to him. He made the final sacrifice, and we are his riches, his inheritance, his joy. Your victory is received in your continuing relationship with Jesus. When you overcome your trials and tribulations, he promises an eternal relationship with him and all your friends who love him.

Jesus, thank you for making it possible for me to be victorious and to reap the rewards you have for me!

NO RESTRAINT

Break forth with dancing!
Make music and sing God's praises with the rhythm of the drums!
PSALM 149:3 TPT

In many countries, people of differing ethnicities have fought bravely for freedom. If they can overcome their enemy and that final victory is won, there are spontaneous responses. People do things without regard for social norms such as kissing a stranger, firing a gun wildly, jumping around like a mad man, yelling expressions of joy. When we claim victory over an oppressor, whether personal or on a large scale, it calls for a huge celebration.

There will be a day when Jesus returns, and we will celebrate in a way beyond our own imaginations. Until that day, we encounter small liberties that can and should be celebrated like our victory over sin, or when a sickness has been healed, or after receiving an answer to months of prayer. When this happens for you, forget societal restraints, and let loose with praise to God. Tell your friends about your victory. Some people may initially be shocked, but there is shared pleasure in seeing a friend set free. Go ahead and openly express your gratitude to God.

God, help me to praise you openly for the moments of joy and victory in my life. I want others to know about you and your goodness.

RECEIVED

All of this is for your benefit. And as God's grace reaches more and more people, there will be great thanksgiving, and God will receive more and more glory.

2 CORINTHIANS 4:15 NLT

Christmas rolls around every year, and we are excited to participate in the giving and receiving of gifts. It is an especially exciting time for younger generations. Remember those days when the tree had so many gifts under it ? We would be so excited about opening the gifts that we didn't take the time to be thankful for what was given. Even as we are older, we sometimes get bigger gifts, and we can forget to be thankful. Most of the time when we are given the one particular gift that we wanted, we express a great deal of pleasure. That's a gift that is well received.

Much like your faith, when you don't take the time to acknowledge what you have been given, and you just take it for granted, your heart can lose sight of what Christ gives each day. When you take the time to enjoy his gifts and to open your heart to him regularly, you are receiving his gift in a way that blesses him.

Jesus, thank you for your gift of life and everlasting treasure. Help me to visit with you every day and to truly enjoy our relationship.

JESUS LEFT HEAVEN

Unto us a Child is born, unto us a Son is given;
and the government will be upon His shoulder.
And His name will be called Wonderful, Counselor, Mighty God,
Everlasting Father, Prince of Peace.
ISAIAH 9:6 NKJV

You may hear this word *incarnation* kicked around in this season. It is a big word meaning that God became a man. It is the process describing how Jesus left heaven, grew in Mary's womb, and was born as an innocent baby. It is the greatest miracle of all. Jesus is fully man and fully God. He now sits at the right hand of the Father, praying for us. He has given us his Holy Spirit who now dwells with us on earth. The Holy Spirit remains with us in order to help us until the final day of our resurrection!

This is the plan of God's salvation, and it starts with the incarnation. It is a great gift to us, and it is why we celebrate with the giving of gifts during this season. You have been given the ultimate gift. Everything else really pales in comparison. As believers in Jesus Christ, we should all be thankful at Christmas time.

Jesus, I am thankful for what you have done. You have given me the greatest gift I can ever have. Thank you!

FOCUS ON PEOPLE

"Look, the virgin shall conceive and bear a son,
and they shall name him Emmanuel,
which means, 'God is with us.'"
MATTHEW 1:23 NRSV

As males we may have trouble naming our emotions. We may, however, have four that we can pretty easily identify: frustration, happiness, sadness, and anger. But there are a great deal more. We are made so that each decision we make has an emotion attached to it. That is because we are made as relational people and emotion is primary to how we live.

Jesus came to be with us not just in his power and with his miracles, but also emotionally. He left his Father's side and entered a sinful world. He was emotionally "in" our troubles and tribulations, as he fully experienced our world. According to the book of Hebrews, Jesus was able to sympathize with our weaknesses in every way except that he did not sin. Like Christ, you can help someone in their troubles. He has equipped you emotionally and spiritually to help those around you.

Jesus, you have helped me by being with me during difficult trials. I want to help others around me. I know that in this season I have been given much, and it is easy to focus on things, but help me focus on caring for the people around me.

SOMEONE HONEST

The king is pleased with words from righteous lips;
he loves those who speak honestly.
PROVERBS 16:13 NLT

When you think of someone who is honest, what comes to mind? Are they authentic, true, and real? Is there anything better than a friend who is honest? This does not mean the kind of "honesty" that is brash, exposing every thought. True honesty in the way that God intends it understands people and is able to speak truth seasoned with compassion. It is a breath of fresh air.

Jesus demonstrated the integrity of an honest person completely. He seasoned his truth with love and understanding. His identity was hidden within his relationship with the Father, so he was sure of himself and did not need the approval of man. When he spoke, it wasn't to manipulate anyone; those who were with him could completely trust his motives. Jesus allows you to be vulnerable with him, and you can trust him. That's also what an honest friend can do for you. Find good friends who are truthful and honest with you and enjoy being with them.

Jesus, help me to be an honest person. Teach me how to live in truth and integrity. Show me how to be real with you and honest about where my heart is.

HUMBLE

"All who exalt themselves will be humbled,
and all who humble themselves will be exalted."
MATTHEW 23:12 NRSV

Pride is pretty tricky. It comes up in all sorts of ways. It can be that we don't want to be told what to do. Or it can be in how well we do something. Other times it comes up when we just start talking about ourselves. The focus of pride is self. And so, when we want to remain humble, we must learn to focus on others. This is why the Bible speaks about looking out for the interests of others and loving one another so much.

Another way of saying this is to stop focusing on yourself. We need to put ourselves in the place where other people can interfere with our lives and be comfortable enough to show their messy sides to us. It is how family works to help us not be prideful. Thank God for your family today. Take time to focus on the things they need and take steps to serve them and love them.

God, you are smart, and I can tell that you know what is best for me. Help me to love my family and to serve others so that I am not focused on myself. Help me with my pride.

HELPER

Many, LORD my God, are the wonders which You have done,
And Your thoughts toward us;
There is none to compare with You.
If I would declare and speak of them,
They would be too numerous to count.

PSALM 40:5 NASB

As you think about the end of this year and the beginning of a new one, it is good to reflect upon the moments you have seen God working in your life. He has been very active in your story even if you have not noticed it. How great is God that he does not get offended at us when we don't see the things he has done! However, we want to take time to sit and think about these things, to thank him, and then ask him to help us in the year to come. He is our rock, and he never fails to be with us. There are none that compare to him.

Think about your year and the things that you want to stop doing, the new things you want to do, and the things you want to keep doing well. This is a business model called "stop, start, and continue," and it helps to evaluate our lives, to thank God for his presence, and to surrender our next year to him.

God, show me the things that I need to stop, start, and continue. I need your help in my life, and I ask for it this coming year.

HAPPY HEART

Since God has shown us great mercy,
I beg you to offer your lives as a living sacrifice to him.
Your offering must be only for God and pleasing to him.
ROMANS 12:1 NCV

He had been away for a week and was looking forward to coming home to his family. His heart was a little heavy. He got home a little later than planned. Opening the door, he was greeted by his mother's warm smile, and the house smelled of a delicious, hot meal. Fresh-baked banana bread, his favorite, was sitting on the counter. The family sat down to eat, and as he closed his eyes in prayer, he was even more pleased to be home. After a satisfying meal, the family played a game and they all talked about his week. As he fell asleep that evening, he told Jesus his week didn't matter, and that his heart was content with what he had.

Have you ever had those times when someone sacrificed themselves to allow you to be pleased? These are the delightful moments in life. Today, find a way to be a pleasing presence to your family.

Jesus, it makes my heart happy to see others smile. I want you to help me to see how I can sacrifice for others so that they know your love.

BELONGING

"Let your light shine before others,
that they may see your good deeds
and glorify your Father in heaven."
MATTHEW 5:16 NIV

What a great word to finish the year and start a new one. You may be reading this by chance, or perhaps if you are a diligent, disciplined person, you have read every one of these devotions. Way to go! Whatever circumstances led you to read this, remember that God has called us first to have faith in his salvation; we cannot earn it. But second, we need to put our faith into action; we cannot have faith without action. This means that we should be actively sharing our faith and showing others why we believe in Jesus Christ. He is our Savior, he loves us excellently, his leadership is perfect, and he is true to himself. There is no other god like him. He is the King of kings and the Lord of lords.

Today as you celebrate the end of this year and the beginning of a new one, remember who you are and who you represent. The greatest lover of humanity, and the mightiest of leaders calls you his son. You belong to Jesus Christ.

Jesus, I believe in you, I belong to you, and I love you. Give me your
strength to finish this year well and to start the new one even stronger!